The **Merchant** of **Venice**
and **Other Stories**
from Shakespeare's Plays

Aksa Karim

misha_syed@hotmail.com

*Oxford Progressive English Readers* provide a wide range of enjoyable reading at six language levels. Text lengths range from 8,000 words at the Starter level, to about 35,000 words at Level 5. The latest methods of text analysis, using specially designed software, ensure that readability is carefully controlled.

The aim of the series is to present stories to engage the interest of the reader; to intrigue, mystify, amuse, delight and stimulate the imagination.

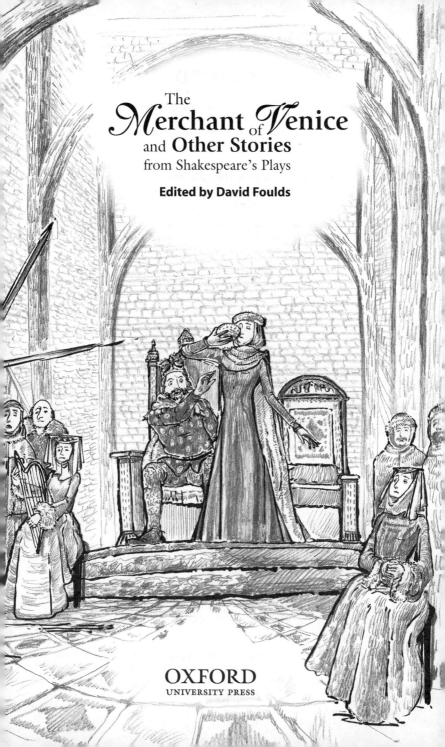

# The
# Merchant of Venice
## and Other Stories
from Shakespeare's Plays

**Edited by David Foulds**

**OXFORD**
UNIVERSITY PRESS

# OXFORD
### UNIVERSITY PRESS

Oxford University Press is a department of the University of Oxford.
It furthers the University's objective of excellence in research, scholarship,
and education by publishing worldwide in

Oxford  New York

Auckland  Cape Town  Dar es Salaam  Hong Kong  Karachi
Kuala Lumpur  Madrid  Melbourne  Mexico City  Nairobi
New Delhi  Shanghai  Taipei  Toronto

With offices in

Argentina  Austria  Brazil  Chile  Czech Republic  France  Greece
Guatemala  Hungary  Italy  Japan  South Korea  Poland  Portugal
Singapore  Switzerland  Thailand  Turkey  Ukraine  Vietnam

Oxford is a registered trade mark of Oxford University Press

First published 1993
Second edition published 2005

This impression (lowest digit)
11  13  15  14  12

Illustrated by Choy Man Yung

Syllabus design and text analysis by David Foulds

ISBN:  978-0-19-597144-6

Printed in Hong Kong
Published by Oxford University Press (China) Ltd
18th Floor, Warwick House East, Taikoo Place, 979 King's Road, Quarry Bay
Hong Kong

# Contents

# Introduction

The stories in this book are taken from plays written by William Shakespeare. They are set in different places hundreds of years ago.

In *The Merchant of Venice*, Antonio is a merchant in the city of Venice in Italy. He is kind and generous and has many friends. His only enemy is a moneylender called Shylock. Antonio's life is in great danger. His friends must find a way to save him ...

In another story, which is set in Scotland, the main character is Macbeth, a nobleman. Under the influence of evil power, he wishes to be king. Because of his desire, many people have to suffer ...

From cold, dark Scotland we move to an island on the warm, blue Mediterranean Sea. Prospero, who knows magic, is waiting for his enemies who put him and his daughter Miranda on this island. What happens when they meet after twelve years?

We then go to the northern part of Europe. Hamlet is the Prince of Denmark. The ghost of Hamlet's father tells Hamlet to take revenge for him. Hamlet is a good, quiet, thoughtful man who does not like fighting. He has a hard time thinking what he should do.

Finally we come to England. Old King Lear asks his three daughters to say how much they love him, so that he can divide his kingdom among them accordingly. Do you think words can prove one's love?

These unusual and surprising stories by Shakespeare tell us about human nature, which has not changed throughout the centuries — how people can be both loving and generous, and cruel and selfish. Some of these stories are tragedies, which are very sad. The rest are comedies, which have a happy ending. You will know which is which after reading them.

## About William Shakespeare

William Shakespeare lived in England over four hundred years ago. He was born in 1564 in Stratford-upon-Avon. He did not go to university. But he studied hard in school when he was small. After he got married and had three children, he moved to London and spent most of his working life there. He died in 1616 (on his 52nd birthday).

Shakespeare is one of the world's greatest writers, and his plays are still enjoyed by millions of people. This is partly because of the wonderful stories they tell. He wrote a total of thirty-eight plays. He also wrote poetry, including many love sonnets. He had a great interest in human nature and all his plays are about this topic. His plays include comedies, romances, histories and tragedies.

Shakespeare spent most of his life writing plays for the theatre, most famously for the Globe Theatre. The Globe Theatre was built in 1598–99. The first recorded performance was of *Julius Caesar* in September 1599. Many of Shakespeare's plays were written for and performed at the Globe, which burnt down in 1613. It was rebuilt in 1614, only to be destroyed by fighting thirty years later. The new Globe Theatre was opened in 1997 about two hundred metres from the original site. It has lime-plastered walls and a thatched roof, just like the original.

# 1

# The Merchant of Venice

## A good friend

In the days when the city of Venice was rich and famous, one of the chief citizens there was a merchant named Antonio. He was a very rich man. He owned many valuable ships and traded with many 5 different foreign countries. He was well known for his kindness, and had many friends. Amongst them was a young Venetian nobleman called Bassanio.

Although he was a nobleman, Bassanio was quite poor. He often spent more money than he had so he 10 could live the way he liked. But Antonio loved him, and always lent him money when he needed it.

Bassanio was in love with a wealthy and noble young lady named Portia, whose father had just died. Portia was not only wealthy, she was beautiful and 15 clever, too. Princes and noblemen were continually asking her to marry them. These men were able to show their wealth and rank by arriving at her house with many servants, and giving her expensive presents. Bassanio didn't have enough money to do this. He was 20 afraid Portia would not consider marrying him because he was so much poorer than all the others.

So one day, Bassanio went to his friend Antonio to ask for his help. He told Antonio that Portia seemed to like him. Bassanio thought that if only he could go to 25 visit her dressed in the finest clothes, with lots of servants, and with some beautiful presents for Portia, he might be successful. If Antonio would lend him enough money, Portia might agree to marry him.

'I am always willing to help you, Bassanio,' said Antonio, 'but I have no money to give you just now. I have used it all to trade with foreign countries. My ships are away at sea at the moment. However, I shall have plenty of money when they come back. Until then, I shall borrow some for you, from Shylock.'

Shylock the Jew was well known in Venice. He was a moneylender, and he had become very wealthy. He loved making more and more money, but he hated spending it.

He was not popular in the city because he was so mean. People who could not pay back the money they owed him got no mercy from Shylock. Antonio had often made it clear to other people that he had no respect for Shylock, because of the way he treated those in debt to him. Antonio himself had many times lent money without asking for any interest, and this spoilt Shylock's business. For these reasons, Shylock hated Antonio, and he was waiting secretly for a chance to harm him.

Bassanio went with Antonio to see Shylock. Antonio asked to borrow 3,000 ducats — a very large amount of money. 'I shall be able to pay it back,' he said to Shylock, 'when my ships return to Venice. They are now at sea and will soon arrive home with many valuable cargoes. As you know, I never lend money for profit myself, or borrow it either, but because Bassanio is my great friend, I will do this for him.'

At first, Shylock seemed unwilling to lend the money. He knew well that what Antonio had said was the truth. 'Your ships may be destroyed by storms before they reach Venice,' he said, 'and then you will be unable to repay me.'

Then he decided to offer Antonio a bargain. 'I am willing to be friends with you, and I will lend you this money for no profit at all. This will show you that I too can be kind and generous, in spite of what you have said about me. But I have an amusing idea, and I hope you will agree to it. If you cannot repay me in time, then you must let me cut a pound of your flesh from any part of your body I choose.'

Bassanio was suspicious of Shylock's intentions, and told Antonio not to accept this plan. But Antonio laughed, and agreed to the joke. Then the three men went to a lawyer to sign the agreement. Antonio took the money from Shylock and gave it to Bassanio, who got ready to visit Belmont, where Portia lived.

## The three boxes

Portia's father had been very anxious that she should choose the best person to be her husband. Before he died, he invented a plan to help her to do this. He had three small metal boxes made. Each one was made of a different metal. The first box was made of gold, the second box of silver, and the third box of lead. One of these boxes contained a picture of Portia. Her father wished her to marry the first man to guess which box contained the picture. Each man must make a promise; if he guessed wrongly, he must never, after that, ask any woman to marry him. Portia felt she must be obedient to her father, even after his death. She was worried that a man she did not like would find the picture, but still she intended to do what her father had asked.

When they heard about this plan, many men did not dare to guess at all, and they went away. They were afraid to lose, because that would mean they would have to stay unmarried for the rest of their lives. This pleased Portia, for she had not liked any of the men who had come to see her. She told her servant, Nerissa, that they were all rather uninteresting, or had no sense of humour, or were always very cross.

One of the men who did dare to choose was a prince from Morocco. He chose the gold box. He thought that only a gold box would be good enough for Portia's picture. Also, there was some writing on the outside of the box. It said: 'The man who chooses this box shall get what many men wish for.'

'Why, that means the lady,' the Prince said to himself. 'All the world desires her. They come from the four corners of the earth, across seas and deserts, just to look at the beautiful Portia. So, if I choose what many men wish for, that surely must mean her picture will be in this box.' But when he opened it, he found only a picture of a skull, to remind him of death, which is what many people wish for when they are old and sick and sad. The Prince was very unhappy.

The next man to guess was the Prince of Aragon from Spain. He did not choose the gold box because he thought the words 'many men' meant all the ordinary people in the world. The Prince of Aragon was a proud man. He would never want what everybody else wanted. Instead he chose the silver box. On the silver box these words were written: 'The man who chooses this box will get what he deserves.' This seemed fair, thought the Prince. He knew that there were people coming to see Portia who were not as good as they seemed. Those people did not deserve to marry Portia. But he was not like them. He was the Prince of Aragon, a very important, rich young man, and he was sure he deserved a wife as good, beautiful and rich as Portia. The Prince was very hopeful when he opened the box. However, inside was not the beautiful picture of Portia that he expected, but the picture of a mad fool. He too went away disappointed.

Then Portia heard that Bassanio had arrived. He had brought with him a friend called Gratiano. Gratiano was in love with Nerissa, Portia's servant, and hoped to persuade Nerissa to marry him while Bassanio was asking Portia to be his wife.

When Bassanio appeared, Portia welcomed him very kindly. She was pleased he had come, as she wanted to marry him. She was very worried that he would choose the wrong box, as the others had done. Portia wanted to help him to find the right one, but she knew she must not. She asked Bassanio to wait some time before he chose, so that they could be together for a while. She knew if he made a mistake and chose the wrong box, they could never be married, and she would never see him again. But Bassanio would not wait; he was anxious to know what would happen. So he was shown the three boxes, of gold, silver and lead.

Bassanio thought for a long time. Finally, he decided. Gold and silver looked precious and beautiful, but many things that were evil, or had no value, could be made to look precious and beautiful. Lead was a plain, ordinary metal. It did not pretend to be better than it was, he thought. It was honest. On the box these words were written: 'The man who chooses this box will be taking a great chance: he might lose everything he has.' That was honest, too, thought Bassanio. So, he chose the lead box.

Portia watched him make the right guess with delight. Bassanio opened the box, and inside it, he saw the picture of Portia. He turned to Portia, and saw that she was as pleased and as happy as he was. She immediately told him that she loved him very much. She then took a ring off her finger and gave it to Bassanio. Portia said that he must never give the ring away; if he did, their love would end. Bassanio accepted the ring happily, and promised never to lose it or give it away. Thus Portia and Bassanio promised to be faithful to each other.

## The trial of Antonio

Gratiano and Nerissa were in the room at the same time, and had been watching what was happening. Gratiano now came forward and said he hoped Portia and Bassanio would be happy. He said that he and Nerissa would like to be married at the same time. Portia and Bassanio were very pleased, and agreed at once.

But then something happened which worried them all a great deal. A messenger arrived with a letter for Bassanio from his friend Antonio, who had borrowed money from Shylock for him. Bassanio's face became pale as he read the letter. It contained very bad news.

Portia quickly asked what had happened. And now, for the first time, Bassanio told her about the money that Antonio had given him. He told her too about Antonio's agreement with Shylock. In this letter, Antonio said that his ships had not come back to port; they had been 5 wrecked at sea and all the valuable goods on them had been lost. Antonio had no money to pay back his debt to Shylock, and the date for him to do this had already passed. He would have to give Shylock a pound of his flesh. 'I am now certain to die, and want to see you,' 10 Antonio wrote.

The messenger told them that Shylock had gone to the Duke of Venice to ask him to deal with the matter. Shylock wanted Antonio to pay him his pound of flesh immediately. And so poor Antonio was now in prison, 15 waiting for his trial.

When Portia heard this terrible story, she wanted to help in any way she could. She offered to pay Shylock much more than the 3,000 ducats he was owed. She told Bassanio to go and help his friend as quickly as 20 possible. However, Portia insisted on one thing: they must be married before Bassanio left Belmont. So all four of them — Portia, Bassanio, Nerissa and Gratiano — went at once to the church and were married. Bassanio and Gratiano then left their wives and went 25 straight back to Venice.

Portia thought a great deal about the problem. She wanted to save Antonio's life, because he had been so generous to her husband, Bassanio. Finally, she wrote a letter to a cousin of hers, who was a well-known and 30 clever lawyer. His name was Dr Bellario. She asked him for his advice, and she also asked him to lend her some lawyer's clothes. Dr Bellario immediately sent her the clothes and told her how Antonio should be defended at his trial. 35

Portia decided what she would do. She told her friends and servants that she was going away for a few quiet days until her husband returned. Then she told Nerissa about her plan. She had decided to go to Venice, and she wanted Nerissa to go with her. However, Portia did not want anyone to recognize her when she was there, so she and Nerissa dressed themselves up in men's clothes. They set off for Venice looking like two young men.

15     Bassanio and Gratiano arrived in Venice, where the trial would soon begin, under the direction of the Duke of Venice. Antonio and Shylock were brought before the Duke. The Duke asked Shylock to give up his cruel demand, and not to take a pound of Antonio's flesh. But
20 Shylock would not agree. 'Antonio had made the promise, and so he must keep it,' he said. Then Bassanio offered to pay Shylock twice as much money as he was owed. Still Shylock would not let Antonio go. 'The laws of Venice allow me to demand a pound of Antonio's
25 flesh, because he has broken our agreement. I hate Antonio, and I will not be persuaded. I would rather have Antonio's flesh than any money I am offered.'

Turning to the Duke, Shylock said, 'Will you permit me to do what I have a right to do, or have you no respect for the laws of Venice?'

## The young lawyer

The Duke had to admit that the law did allow Shylock to refuse the money instead of Antonio's flesh. He liked Antonio, but did not dare to treat him differently from any other citizen. The law said that anyone who makes an agreement must keep it. If Shylock insisted, Antonio would have to die. Shylock did insist. He thought to himself, 'At last I shall be able to treat Antonio in the way he deserves. I do not pity him at all. This proud merchant always hated me and made others hate me too. I will not forgive him.'

The Duke had already written to a famous lawyer asking him to come to Venice to advise him about this difficult problem. The man to whom he had written was Dr Bellario — Portia's cousin, who had shown her how Antonio could be defended. As Shylock would not show any mercy to Antonio, the Duke decided to wait for Dr Bellario. 'Perhaps this clever lawyer can find a way to save Antonio's life,' he thought.

Just as the Duke decided to do this, a clerk came in. He said he had brought a letter from Dr Bellario. In this letter, Dr Bellario wrote that he was ill, and would not be able to come to the trial. However, he asked if a young lawyer friend of his could come instead. The Duke agreed to do as Dr Bellario asked, and he invited the young lawyer to come in.

The clerk who brought the letter for the Duke was really Nerissa, dressed as a man. The young lawyer was really Portia, who was dressed in the lawyer's clothes that Dr Bellario had lent her. The Duke was surprised when he saw how young the lawyer was, but he asked him to defend Antonio.

Portia turned to Shylock and asked him to show mercy to Antonio. 'Mercy,' she said, 'rewards not only the man who receives it, but also the man who gives it. We pray to God, hoping he will show us mercy, and we should show mercy to other people.' But Shylock would not listen to her.

'I only ask to be paid what I am owed,' he said.

'Can he pay back the money you lent him?' asked Portia.

Bassanio quickly said, 'He can pay it, and he is willing to pay more. I can pay ten times as much for Antonio.' Bassanio begged the lawyer to forget about the exact words of the law, in order to save a life.

'No,' said Portia, 'I cannot allow that. If we do not insist that this man obeys the law now, other people may follow his bad example, and the whole country will suffer.'

Shylock was delighted when he heard this answer. 'Oh, what a wise young judge!' he cried happily. He expected the trial to end very soon. He praised the young lawyer and laughed at Antonio. Portia then asked to see the agreement Antonio and Shylock had signed. She read it, and agreed that Shylock could have his pound of flesh. Then Portia turned to Antonio and commanded him to uncover his chest. Shylock was ready to kill Antonio. He called out, 'Oh, noble judge! Oh, wonderful young man!'

Antonio thought he was going to die. He said goodbye to his friend Bassanio, and asked him to tell Portia why he had died. Bassanio was very unhappy, and he replied that he would give anything he had to save Antonio if he could. He would even be willing to lose his own life to help Antonio.

'Now,' said Portia to Shylock, 'take the pound of flesh that is owed to you. Cut it from this man's chest.'

Shylock had his knife in his hand as he moved forward. He was ready to cut out Antonio's heart. 'Oh, wise judge! Oh, wise young judge!' he cried. To Antonio he cried, 'Prepare yourself!' 5

## Shylock is defeated

Before he could use his knife to make even the smallest cut in Antonio's skin, Portia stopped him.

'Wait!' she said. 'I have something else to say. The 10 words of this agreement say clearly that you may take "a pound of flesh". But there is nothing in it to say that you may take even one drop of blood. Antonio's flesh you may take, but if you spill a single drop of blood, then all your property 15 must be given to the State. That is the law of Venice.'

Shylock stood completely still. He was so surprised and annoyed he could hardly speak. 'Is that what the law commands?' he asked. Portia offered to show him the law on the subject. Gratiano could see how angry
5  Shylock was, and now he cried out, 'Oh, wise judge! See, Shylock, what a wise judge he is!'

Shylock then remembered that Bassanio had offered to pay back the money, and even to pay him more. 'I will accept your offer,' he said to Bassanio. 'Pay back
10  three times as much as I lent Antonio, and then I will let him go.'

'Here it is,' said Bassanio, holding out the money. But Portia would not allow this. A little while ago, Shylock had refused the money, so now he should have
15  nothing, she said.

Shylock, very angry, was about to leave, when Portia called him back. 'Wait!' she said. 'There is another law we must remember. If anyone plans to kill a citizen of Venice, half his property must be given to that citizen.
20  The other half must be given to the State. And the Duke may order any other punishment he thinks is right. Kneel in front of him and pray for mercy.'

Shylock had so recently refused mercy to Antonio that he could not now expect mercy for himself. But the
25  Duke was not as cruel as the moneylender.

'I will show you that men can be much kinder to each other than you think. You will not lose your life; I will tell you this even before you ask me to save you. But you must give half your money and property to
30  Antonio, and half to the State.'

And now Antonio showed mercy to the moneylender. 'I will not take my share of Shylock's wealth. But he must become a Christian,' he said.

Shylock was also forced to sign a will. This will said
35  that Jessica, his daughter, and Lorenzo, her husband,

should receive all of Shylock's money when he died. Lorenzo was a good friend of Antonio's. Not long ago, Jessica had run away from her father and secretly married Lorenzo, a Christian. She had taken some money and jewels with her when she left home, and Shylock had been very angry. At first he could only shout, 'My daughter! Oh, my money! Oh, my daughter! She has run away with a Christian! How can the law help me now? Oh, my money, my daughter!' Shylock seemed to be just as worried about his money as he was about his daughter. The moneylender had said that he would not leave Jessica any money when he died, and he would never forgive her.

The Jew now knew that he must obey Portia's and Antonio's commands. 'I am ill,' he cried. 'Let me go home. Send the agreement to my house. I will sign it.'

So the Duke let Shylock go, and the trial ended.

## Portia's trick

During the trial, everyone had been very surprised to see how young and wise the lawyer was. But no one had suspected that the lawyer was really Portia. Even Bassanio had not guessed. Portia had changed her appearance and voice so cleverly that her own husband could not recognize her.

Bassanio and Antonio wanted to show the young lawyer that they were very grateful for his help. 'Please accept the 3,000 ducats owed to Shylock,' Antonio said. But Portia would not accept the money. Bassanio was also very anxious to give the lawyer something. So Portia thought she would trick her husband, for a joke. 'If you insist, give me your gloves,' she told Bassanio. Bassanio took off his gloves, showing the ring on his hand. 'As a sign of your thankfulness, give me that ring

on your finger.' Bassanio immediately drew his hand away. This ring was the one Portia had given him when she promised to marry him. He had promised never to give it away. He pretended that the ring had no value,
5 and was too small to give as a present. But Portia asked for it again. Bassanio then told her it was his wife's ring, and she had made him promise never to give it away.

'That is a common excuse,' replied Portia. 'That is what men say when they do not want to give a present.
10 Your wife will not be angry with you for long. You can tell her how much I deserved the ring.'

Portia and Nerissa, still dressed as a lawyer and a clerk, turned to go. Almost immediately, Antonio persuaded Bassanio to give up the ring. Bassanio felt
15 ashamed to seem ungrateful, so he gave it to Portia. Nerissa also cleverly managed to persuade Gratiano to give her the ring that she had given to him. He too had promised never to give it away.

Portia and Nerissa left Venice, and went as quickly
20 as possible to Belmont. They wanted to get there before their husbands returned. When they got back to Portia's house, they changed their clothes at once. Soon they were sitting down, dressed in their ordinary clothes, waiting for their husbands to come back to them. Not
25 long after, the two men arrived, with Antonio. Bassanio introduced Antonio to his wife. 'This is the friend,' he told her, 'who has helped me so much.' So Portia welcomed Antonio to her house.

While she was doing this, she saw Gratiano and
30 Nerissa quarrelling in a corner of the room. 'What is happening?' cried Portia. 'Are you quarrelling already? What is the matter?'

'We are arguing about a ring which Nerissa gave me,' Gratiano explained. 'The ring had these words written
35 on it: "Love me and never leave me".'

'I am annoyed because Gratiano promised faithfully that he would keep it,' Nerissa said, 'and now he has given it away to a lawyer's clerk. It does not matter whether it was a valuable ring or not. He should not have given it away.'                                    5

## Everything is put right again

Portia was now determined to enjoy the trick she had played on her husband. 'Of course Gratiano was wrong to give away his wife's first present. I, too, gave my husband a ring, and made him promise to keep it. If he    10
gave that ring away, I would be very angry with him indeed.'

Then Gratiano replied, 'But Bassanio did give his ring away — he gave it to the young lawyer who asked for it. And then the boy, his clerk, asked me for my ring.'    15

When she heard this, Portia pretended to be very angry. She asked Bassanio, 'Which ring did you give him? I hope it was not the ring that you accepted from me.'

Bassanio felt very unhappy when he saw how angry    20
his wife was. But he had to admit the truth, and tell her that he had given the ring away. 'I wish you knew how unwilling I was to give the ring to this man, and why I gave it to him.'

But Portia still pretended to be angry. She accused    25
him of giving the ring to a woman. Bassanio thought Portia must think he was very unkind. He told her he had given the lawyer the ring because he was so grateful to him for saving Antonio's life. 'If you had been there,' he said, 'I think you would have told me to    30
give him the ring.'

Then Antonio turned to Portia and said, 'These unhappy quarrels have all been caused by me!'

'Do not treat this matter so seriously,' replied Portia. She took the ring from her bag and said, 'Give him this ring, and tell him to keep it better than he kept the last one.'

5     Antonio passed the ring to Bassanio, who looked at it. He was surprised to see that it was the one he had given away. Portia then showed her husband the letter from Dr Bellario, and so he discovered that the clever lawyer was really Portia, his wife. Bassanio realized

10 that his own wife's courage and cleverness had saved the life of his dear friend Antonio. He was surprised and delighted.

    Soon afterwards, Antonio received good news about his own affairs. Portia handed him some letters which

15 had just arrived. These told Antonio that the ships which he thought were lost had returned to Venice, and had brought back their valuable cargoes. Antonio was a wealthy man again.

    Thus the story of the Merchant of Venice ended —

20 with good news for the merchant, and with laughter between the husbands and wives over the joke about the rings.

# 2
# Macbeth

## The Thane of Glamis

Macbeth was a great Scottish nobleman, who commanded the army of King Duncan of Scotland. He was called the Thane of Glamis, and he belonged to the same family as the King.

King Duncan argued with some of his noblemen. They refused to obey him as their ruler, and a war broke out between them. The noblemen were helped by the King of Norway, who landed in Scotland with an army to fight King Duncan. King Duncan sent Macbeth and Banquo, two of his most faithful generals, to attack the disobedient noblemen.

After a terrible fight, King Duncan's men defeated their enemies, and the King of Norway was forced to ask for peace. In the battle, Macbeth fought with great bravery; all the soldiers and messengers talked about him and praised his conduct. King Duncan wanted to reward him by giving him a new honour.

The two generals, Macbeth and Banquo, were returning from the battle across a wild and lonely part of the country. Suddenly, three evil-looking old women appeared in front of them. These old women were witches. Macbeth was frightened by this awful sight, and he asked the witches who they were. The answer he received from the first witch was, 'Welcome, Macbeth! Welcome, Thane of Glamis!' The second witch cried, 'Welcome, Macbeth! Welcome, Thane of Cawdor!' The third witch cried, 'Welcome, Macbeth! Welcome the man who will be king!'

Macbeth did not understand these words. He was the Thane of Glamis, but he knew he was not the Thane of Cawdor, and he knew he was not the king. He was so shocked by this that he could not speak. The witches then turned to Banquo and spoke to him. 'You are less important than Macbeth, and yet more important. You will not be so happy, and yet you will be happier. Your children will be kings, though you will not.'

Macbeth wanted the witches to tell him what their words meant, but it was too late; they disappeared as quickly as they had come.

As Macbeth and Banquo stood discussing these strange words, two noblemen sent by King Duncan rode up to them to praise them for their victory. They told Macbeth that the King wished to reward him for fighting so well in the battle, and had therefore given him a new title, which was 'Thane of Cawdor'. Macbeth could not believe what he heard. When he was sure it was true, he began to think about the other words the witches had spoken. Could he really become King of Scotland? Banquo remained calm, and warned Macbeth not to trust the witches too much. He realized that Macbeth was allowing himself to think dangerous and wild thoughts. But Macbeth could not stop thinking about what the witches had said. He wondered what he could do to make their words come true. He was shocked by the ideas he had. Perhaps, after all, if it was his fortune to be king, there would be no need for him to do anything.

After Macbeth's victory, King Duncan told him that he would like to visit his castle. This would be a great honour for Macbeth. When Macbeth heard this, he asked to be allowed to go home at once to prepare for the royal visit. Before he set off, he sent a letter to his wife, Lady Macbeth. In this letter he told her about

the witches, and what they had
said. He also told her that some of the
witches' words had already come true. He
encouraged his wife to believe that she might one
day be Queen of Scotland. From that day on, Macbeth    5
could think of nothing else. When Duncan told
everyone·that his elder son, Malcolm, would be king
after him, Macbeth wondered how he could deal with
this difficulty.

## Lady Macbeth

When Lady Macbeth read her husband's letter, she was determined that he should rule Scotland. She was sure that Macbeth would have to act without mercy for
5 others. He would have to make himself king, but she was afraid he was too kind to do it. Lady Macbeth knew that her husband would love to be king, but she also realized that she would have to urge him to take action. She decided that Duncan must be murdered while he
10 was staying with them at their castle that night. Lady Macbeth did not believe anyone would discover who had killed the King. She was certain that Macbeth was so well loved and admired that no one would think that he had done it.

15 As soon as Macbeth came home, she told him about her plan. She advised him to show no sign that anything was wrong, and to welcome his guests cheerfully. She said he did not need to do any more than that. 'Leave the rest to me,' she said.

20 The King arrived, and was welcomed by Lady Macbeth with great respect. Duncan was pleased. The castle garden seemed calm and beautiful after the battle, and it was very pleasant to rest and to be among friends. Here he thought he could forget, for a while,
25 the troubles of his kingdom. He had supper with Macbeth, who showed him the room where he would sleep. When the King went to bed, he felt peaceful and happy. He was so pleased with everything about his visit that he sent a wonderful diamond to Lady
30 Macbeth as a present.

Macbeth felt neither calm nor peaceful. He was sure he could not murder the King. He could not kill one of his own relatives, a guest in his own castle. He was responsible for Duncan's safety because the King was his guest. Besides, he was such a good and fair king that it seemed very wicked to kill him.

While Macbeth was considering what to do, Lady Macbeth came into the room. He told her he could not kill Duncan. 'The King has given me great honours already, and I am very popular with the people. I am grateful for this; it is enough for me,' he said.

Lady Macbeth told him that she would never respect him again, and that she would always think of him as a coward. She told him that they would certainly succeed if they were determined enough. She explained to him how easy it would be to murder Duncan without anyone ever finding out about it. Macbeth changed his mind, and agreed to do everything that his wife suggested. She said that she would give some wine to the two guards at the door of Duncan's room. She would put a drug in the wine, and this would make them fall asleep very quickly. Then it would be easy for Macbeth to get past the guards and murder Duncan while the King was sleeping. Later, they could blame the guards for committing the crime.

## The murder of Duncan

Later that night, when the guests were in bed and the castle was quiet, Lady Macbeth went to the King's room. She gave the drugged wine to the guards, and they soon fell asleep. She took their daggers and placed them where Macbeth would find them. Lady Macbeth felt brave enough to kill Duncan herself and went into his room. However, when she saw the King lying on his bed, asleep, he looked like her dead father, and she could not do anything to harm him. She returned to her room and waited for her husband to go and do the deed.

Macbeth crept through
the dark and silent castle. Suddenly,
he saw a terrible sight. A knife, covered
in blood, appeared before his eyes. The handle was
5  turned towards his hand. He stretched out his hand to
take it, but it was not real. He realized that thinking
about the murder of the King was affecting his mind.

He heard a bell ring. It was Lady Macbeth, in her
room, letting Macbeth know that she had prepared
10  everything. Now was the time to act. Macbeth went on
towards Duncan's room. He was even more frightened
than before. The two guards at the door were fast
asleep, and so was the King himself. It was easy for
Macbeth to go in. No one would ever have guessed that
15  Duncan's most faithful commander was going to kill
him. It did not take Macbeth more than a few seconds
to do the awful deed.

After killing Duncan, as Macbeth moved back
towards the door, he heard one of the guards laughing
20  in his sleep. The other servant cried out 'Murder!' but
he, too, was asleep, and only dreaming. Then they both
woke up, but they did not see Macbeth there, and they
did not know that anything was wrong. They soon went
back to sleep.

In her room, Lady Macbeth waited anxiously for her husband to return. She listened to every sound, and when she heard some noises coming from the King's room, she thought Macbeth had failed. But at that moment he returned, and told her he had done the terrible deed.

Although he had killed the King, Macbeth was a very frightened man. He knew his peace and happiness had been destroyed for ever by that crime. He was very shocked, and dared not think about what he had done. He told his wife he thought he could hear a voice shouting out, 'Sleep no more — Macbeth shall sleep no more, because he has murdered innocent sleep.'

His wife scolded him for his weakness and for bringing the guards' daggers back from Duncan's room. They were covered in blood. She told him to go back and put them beside the guards, and to wipe some of Duncan's blood on their clothes. Then everyone would think they were the murderers. Macbeth did not dare to go back and see what he had done, so Lady Macbeth went instead.

Macbeth could not rest. His mind was full of wild thoughts and fears. Every noise he heard frightened him. He kept on staring at his hands, which were covered with blood. He imagined that they would never be clean again. He thought there could not be enough water in all the seas to wash that blood away. Instead, he thought, the blood on his hands would turn the green seas red.

Lady Macbeth returned. Her hands were now covered with blood, too, but she told her husband, 'A little water will clear away this deed. How easy it is then!' She told him to go to bed as if nothing had happened. People would be suspicious if they were found awake and dressed in the middle of the night.

# The new King of Scotland

Early the next morning, there was a loud knocking at the castle gates. Two of Duncan's noblemen, Macduff and Lennox, had come to offer their services to Duncan. Macbeth went to welcome them.

They told him that where they had been staying that night, the weather had been very wild and stormy. The wind was so strong, it had blown the chimneys down. People heard strange noises in the air, like the sound of people crying, and the terrible screams of people dying. Some said they had felt the earth shaking.

While they were speaking, the terrible murder was discovered. Soon, everyone in the castle knew the dreadful news. Macbeth and Lady Macbeth both pretended to be very shocked. When Macbeth was told of the murder, he went straight to the King's room. He found the King's two servants there. Their hands and faces were covered with blood, and their daggers, unwiped, were lying where they had been sleeping. They could not understand what had happened, and stared at each other in confusion. Macbeth killed them immediately.

When he returned, he said he was sorry he had killed the servants, but that his feelings of love for the King had been too strong for him. He could not stop himself from killing the King's murderers when he saw them standing there with Duncan's blood on their clothes, and on their daggers. Of course, Macbeth hoped to hide his own guilt by doing this.

Lady Macbeth pretended to be so shocked when she heard the news that she became ill, and had to be helped from the room.

Duncan's sons, Malcolm and Donalbain, were staying at Macbeth's castle. They decided to run away.

They did not think that their lives would be safe if they remained in Scotland. They thought that the person who had killed Duncan in order to be king would surely try to kill his sons, too, because they ought to be king after him. One of them went to England, the other     5
to Ireland. They left so quickly that some people were certain they must be the ones who had killed the King.

Macbeth was then the nearest relative to Duncan left in Scotland, and so everyone agreed that he should be king. The words of the witches had come true.     10

## Banquo's ghost

Although he was now king, Macbeth did not feel safe. After his terrible crime, he could not trust anyone, not even his oldest friends. He was most afraid of Banquo, who had been with him when the witches spoke to     15
him. Banquo knew that Macbeth had been excited by the witches' words, and that he really wanted to be king. Besides, the witches had said that the kingdom would one day be ruled by Banquo's family. This thought made Macbeth both angry and afraid. He had     20
risked his own life when he murdered Duncan. He wondered whether he had helped Banquo even more than himself. Macbeth felt that he could not safely allow him to live, and he decided to murder Banquo's son also. He was so frightened and so determined not to     25
lose the kingdom he had just won, that he planned to commit murder again.

In order to kill Banquo, the new King and Queen gave a great feast for the chief noblemen. They invited Banquo and his son, Fleance, as the most important     30
guests. That day, Banquo and Fleance went out riding but, on their way back to Macbeth's castle, they were attacked by three men. Macbeth had paid these men to

kill Banquo and Fleance but, in the struggle, Fleance
escaped. Though Banquo was murdered, his son
managed to get to England, and Banquo's family did,
later, become Kings of Scotland. In spite of all
5 Macbeth's plans, the things the witches said to Banquo
came true.

The time for the feast arrived, and the King and
Queen sat down happily with their guests. The Queen
welcomed everyone, and was determined to delight
10 her guests. Macbeth talked freely with the noblemen,
and everyone was pleased with the feast. Macbeth said
cheerfully that he hoped his two chief guests would
soon arrive.

Suddenly, he rose from his seat, trembling with fear.
15 All the visitors noticed, and wondered what had
happened. Macbeth thought he could see Banquo,
sitting in the chair that had been kept for him,
but no one else could see anything.
Lady Macbeth tried to calm
20 her anxious guests.

She assured them that Macbeth was not really ill. Turning to him, she told him fiercely to control his fear before everyone guessed their secret. At that moment, Banquo's ghost seemed to disappear. Macbeth, with more courage now, sat down again. He drank some wine, and wished all his visitors, including Banquo, good health. When he said, 'We miss our dear friend Banquo, and wish that he were here,' Banquo's ghost appeared again. Macbeth was helpless with fear and could not bear the terrible sight. He cried out in a loud voice to the ghost to go away.

Everyone got up, wondering whether Macbeth had gone mad. They could see nothing. The Queen quickly asked her guests to leave, in case Macbeth said even more suspicious things. She told them that Macbeth's behaviour was not unusual, and that these fears did not last for very long. However, Lennox and some other noblemen did not forget what had happened, and were suspicious of Macbeth's strange behaviour. Macduff had not even come to the feast, because he was afraid it might be some kind of trap for the King's enemies.

Macbeth was afraid, too; many noblemen did not trust him, and Fleance was alive in England. He was prepared to kill anyone to defend his position. He decided to ask the advice of the three witches again — they seemed to know about everything that would happen.

## Macbeth's cruelty

Early the next day, Macbeth went to the lonely place where he had met the witches. He found them preparing magic mixtures from parts of animals and plants. They used these secret mixtures to obtain knowledge of future events. Macbeth asked them to tell him what would happen to him, and immediately he saw three devils in front of him. The first was in the form of a head wearing a battle helmet. Macbeth began to speak to it, but the witches told him to be silent. Then the head slowly said, 'Macbeth! Macbeth! Macbeth! Watch Macduff! Watch the Thane of Fife!' After this, the head disappeared into the ground.

The second devil appeared to the noise of thunder. It was in the form of a child covered in blood. It told Macbeth to be very cruel, bold and determined, and to fear no one. There was no one born of a woman who could harm him. Macbeth at once thought of the warning he had just received about Macduff. 'I need not fear him, then,' he thought. But he decided that he would kill Macduff anyway, to be quite safe.

Then a third devil appeared. It was a child dressed like a king, with a tree in its hand. It said, 'Macbeth shall never lose a battle until great Birnam Wood moves towards Dunsinane Hill!'

'That will never happen,' said Macbeth to himself. He was encouraged by these words. He believed all he had heard, and he felt he need never fear his enemies again.

Before Macbeth left the place, he asked the witches whether any of Banquo's children would ever become kings of Scotland. This was the one problem that still worried him. The three old women warned him not to ask this, but he insisted. He heard music and, one by one, eight shadows passed by him. They were the shadows of kings. The last one was Banquo, covered in blood, who turned his head and smiled at Macbeth. He 5 was holding a mirror in his hand in which Macbeth could see still more kings. These were all the children of Banquo, and would rule Scotland after Macbeth. Macbeth was very shocked, and cried, 'This is a terrible sight! Now I see what it means, for Banquo is pointing 10 to the kings in the mirror to show that they are his children. Will this really happen?' The witches assured him that it would, and then the sound of the music faded away and they disappeared.

As Macbeth was returning from the witches, he met 15 one of his noblemen. This man told him that Macduff had left his home and family suddenly, and had gone to England to join Malcolm, Duncan's son. Malcolm hoped to gather an army to defeat Macbeth. Then he could become King of Scotland, as his father had 20 planned. Macbeth was very angry when he heard this news. He attacked Macduff's castle, and savagely killed his wife and all his children.

This deed, and other actions like it, did little to help Macbeth. Many of his noblemen and soldiers hated him 25 for his unnecessary cruelty. Some left him and joined his enemies. Those who stayed with him did not respect or admire him any longer. Macbeth himself was always anxious and unhappy.

## The death of Lady Macbeth 30

The Queen suffered from terrible dreams because of her guilt. Her servants often found her walking around the castle in her sleep, talking wildly about the murder.

One night, a doctor and one of the Queen's ladies were talking about her. The lady was saying how one night she had seen the Queen get out of bed, put on a warm coat, and then go to her desk, unlock it, and take out some paper. She wrote a letter, read what she had written, folded it, and put it away in the desk, and then returned to bed — yet the whole time she was fast asleep.

As they were talking, the Queen walked past. She was carrying a lighted candle. Her eyes were wide open, but she was asleep. Then she stopped, put the candle down, and began to rub her hands.

The lady said she had often seen the Queen do that. It looked as if she were washing her hands. She would do it for a quarter of an hour without stopping.

'There is a spot of blood here,' Lady Macbeth said suddenly.

She spoke aloud, but she was talking to herself. She rubbed her hands harder. 'Oh, go away, dreadful spot!' she cried. 'Will my hands never be clean?'

She lifted one of her hands to her face. 'There is still the smell of blood here,' she said. 'Oh, all the perfume in the world will never make this little hand smell sweet again.' And then she began to cry loudly in fear and horror. After a while she became quieter. She spoke some more, as if she were talking to Macbeth. Then she went back to bed. All this time, she had seemed to be awake, but she was really asleep.

A few days later, Lady Macbeth was dead. Many people said she killed herself.

## The moving wood

Macbeth tried to gather an army to fight Malcolm, but he had no friends left, and no one wanted to help him. He began to wish he were dead, but he had enough courage left to come out of his castle at Dunsinane and fight a hopeless battle against his enemies.

While Macbeth was preparing for the battle, a messenger came to tell him that he had seen a strange sight. 'As I was watching on the hill for the enemy, I looked towards Birnam, and I thought the wood began to move.'

'You are a liar and a slave!' cried the King. Then he added, 'If you are lying, I will hang you from the nearest tree. But if your story is true, I do not care if you hang me instead.' He thought to himself, 'Now I doubt the advice of the witches, who spoke the truth, but tricked me all the time. The words of those devils never mean what they seem to mean.'

Then Macbeth went out to meet his enemy. The messenger had not lied. When Malcolm's army was

marching through Birnam Wood, he ordered each man to cut down a branch and carry it with him. Thus Macbeth would find it much more difficult to estimate the size of the attacking army. The result was that the
5 whole of Birnam Wood seemed to be moving towards Dunsinane.

In spite of his hopeless situation, Macbeth fought fiercely and with great courage. He remembered that the witches had said that no one born of a woman could
10 harm him, and this increased his bravery. He killed many of his enemies, although his own small army did not support him well.

Meanwhile, Macduff, who was leading the first part of Malcolm's army, was determined to fight Macbeth.
15 He wished to kill the King himself, because Macbeth had murdered his family. At last the two men saw each other. Macbeth did not want to fight, but Macduff rushed towards him, and a fierce struggle began. Macduff fought savagely, thinking of his dead family,
20 but Macbeth was not at all afraid. He told Macduff that his life was protected against anyone who had been born of a woman. Macduff replied that he had not been born of a woman in the ordinary way, but had been taken from his mother's body before the proper time.
25 For a moment, Macbeth's courage disappeared. 'I will not fight you, then,' he cried to Macduff.

Macduff laughed. 'Live, then, a prisoner, and see all men laugh at you as a coward!'

Macbeth thought for a moment, and then replied, 'I
30 will never obey young Malcolm, or be cursed by the people. Let us fight, Macduff!'

After a great struggle, Macduff killed the King, and cut off his head. He presented it to Malcolm, the new King. Everyone was relieved that the reign of the cruel
35 King Macbeth had ended.

# 3

# The Tempest

## A frightening storm

The beautiful, blue Mediterranean Sea was clear and
calm. Far from land, driven along by a gentle wind,
a ship was sailing slowly to the north. It had come from
Tunis, on the coast of Africa, and was going home to ⁵
Naples in the south of Italy. It was passing a small,
unimportant looking island, a little way to the west.

Suddenly, as if by magic, the weather changed. Dark
clouds began to gather, lightning started to flash,
thunder crashed, and rain poured down. The wind ¹⁰
roared, and blew harder and harder every minute, one
moment from one direction, the next from another. The
waves grew higher and higher, and broke like huge
waterfalls over the ship. Out of the darkness,
strange flames began to appear, and ¹⁵
soon it looked as if the ship were
burning. It was very frightening.

The sailors did not know what was happening. They ran about in the wind and rain, this way and that, pulling up some sails, and letting down others. But nothing they did would get them away from this terrible storm.

Slowly, the ship was blown towards the island. Before long it seemed as if it would hit the rocks and break up. The sailors and all the people on board would be thrown into the sea, and drown. Many of the passengers were so afraid that they did not wait for the ship to reach the rocks. They jumped into the rough water, hoping they would be able to save themselves by swimming to the island.

On the island, two people were watching the ship fighting its way through the high, wild waves. One was a young girl, called Miranda. She was about fifteen years old and very beautiful. With Miranda was her father, Prospero. Prospero was a tall, old man. He had grey hair and a grey beard, and a wise, old face. But he was not an ordinary old man. He was a powerful magician. In fact, Prospero had caused the storm.

Miranda thought the ship was going to sink, and she felt very sorry for the men in it. She asked her father to use his magic powers to calm the sea and save the ship if he could. Prospero told her not to be anxious, for no one would be harmed. He said that he had a good reason for causing the storm and making the ship come to the island.

'But now,' he added, 'I have something to tell you, before I let you know why I have made this storm. I must explain to you how you and I came here, twelve years ago, and where we came from. I have not spoken to you about this before, but now the time has come to tell you all about it. Please sit down and listen carefully.'

## Prospero's story

Miranda was very pleased to learn that she was going to hear the story of her past. She could remember, when she was a tiny child, having lots of women around her to serve her. Now she and her father lived almost alone  5 on this small island. There was only one other human there, and he was an ugly, stupid person called Caliban, who worked for them as a servant.

Miranda often wondered about the women she remembered. Her life, when she was a little girl, must  10 have been very different to the way it was now. What had happened to make it change so much? She sat down and listened carefully.

'Twelve years ago,' said Prospero, 'when you were just a small child, I was the ruler of Milan, in Italy. I had  15 money and lands and power. But I was not interested in those things, or in doing the work of government. I preferred to study my books. I asked my brother, Antonio, to look after the government of Milan for me, but I should not have trusted him so much.  20

'Antonio did not just want to govern for me, he wanted to be the ruler himself. He planned to kill me, and he persuaded the King of Naples, Alonso, to help him. One dark night, their servants seized you and me, and put us on a ship. We were taken a long way out to  25 sea, and when we were far away from any land, they made us get into an old boat. It was so old and so small, it looked as if it would soon break into pieces. They left us on that little boat. They hoped it would sink, and we would drown.  30

'A man called Gonzalo was ordered to do these things for my brother Antonio and King Alonso. But Gonzalo was a kind man. He did not like what the King and my brother made him do. He had to obey them, but

he tried to help us. He put some water, food and clothes in the boat with us. Knowing that I loved my books more than anything else, he had gone to my library and taken the most valuable ones he could find. He put
5 those in the boat, too.'

## The island

'That little boat was stronger than it looked. We sailed in it for many days across the stormy waters. In the end, a long way from our home in Italy, it brought us to this
10 island where we now live.

'At first, the island seemed a strange and mysterious place. It had once been controlled by the magic power of an evil old witch called Sycorax. But she had died long before our boat brought us here. The only human
15 we found here was her son, Caliban, though he is so strange and ugly, it is still hard to think of him as a human being. I tried to help Caliban, but he was too stupid to learn anything, so I let him live with us as our servant.

20 'I found the large, dry cave which is now our house. There I put my books. Every day I read them, and studied them carefully, until I became very skilful in magic, and much stronger than the old witch, Sycorax, ever was. And so we have lived here quietly ever since
25 — you, me and Caliban, our servant.

'But now, Miranda, my dear daughter, at last, the time has come for our lives to change. The men on that ship out there are my old enemies. They passed by this island by a strange chance. Alonso, the King of Naples,
30 arranged for his daughter, Claribel, to marry the King of Tunis. They have just been to the wedding in Tunis, and Alonso and his noble friends are returning home to Italy. With the King is my unfaithful brother, Antonio,

now the ruler of Milan. King Alonso's brother, Sebastian, is there too, as is Alonso's son, Ferdinand, and the kind old man, Gonzalo.

'I have used my magic to make a storm so that the ship will come towards this island. I want to bring my old enemies here, so that they will be in my power.' 5

By the time Prospero had finished his story, the storm had stopped, and the sea was clear and calm again. The ship was nowhere to be seen. However, although Prospero had made the storm on purpose, it 10 was not his plan to harm his enemies. In fact, his intention was quite different. He planned to use his magic to make Antonio and King Alonso feel sorry for their evil deeds. Then he planned to forgive them, so that they would no longer be his enemies. 15

## Ariel

Miranda, Prospero and their servant, Caliban, were the only three humans on the island, but there were many spirits living there. These were magic creatures who could change their appearance and become invisible, 20 and do many things that human beings usually cannot do. Prospero was such a great magician that he could command them all.

Prospero's skill in magic had given him power over all the island. He used the magic to help many good 25 spirits who had been trapped by Sycorax. She had caught the good spirits, who refused to obey her evil commands, and put them inside trees. Prospero had let them out of their tree prisons, and now these spirits loved him and served him gratefully. 30

Ariel was the chief of these spirits. He was always ready when his master, Prospero, called him. He was able to fly through the air without anyone seeing him, and could do many other strange things. For example, he could change himself into different shapes and make himself look like a bear or any other animal. Ariel was always very cheerful and full of life, but he also liked to play all sorts of tricks on people. He loved playing tricks on the stupid Caliban when he was lazy and did not obey Prospero's orders.

Ariel had been following Prospero's orders, and helping him make the storm. When Prospero called the faithful Ariel to him, he told Prospero about everything that he had done. He said that he had frightened the passengers on the ship with all kinds of tricks so that they had jumped into the sea. Ferdinand, the son of the King of Naples, had jumped in first, and had swum safely to the shore. He was quite near to where Prospero and Miranda were. Everyone else was safe; the sailors were asleep on the ship, and the other passengers had landed on different parts of the island. However, each group of passengers thought that all the others had drowned. Ferdinand was sitting alone on the shore, weeping about his father's death. His father was somewhere else, with a few friends, weeping about the loss of his dear son.

Prospero was very pleased with what Ariel had done. There was a lot more work to do, and because Prospero was such a great magician, Ariel had to obey him and work very hard. But Prospero knew that Ariel wanted to be completely free more than anything else in the world. He promised the little spirit that if everything went well, there would never be any more work to do after that, and he would give him his freedom. Prospero asked Ariel to make himself invisible so that no one could see him except the great magician himself. Then he gave him something else to do.

## Miranda falls in love

Not long afterwards, some music and singing could be heard. It was Ariel and some of the other spirits, but as no one could see them, the music seemed very strange. Ferdinand, King Alonso's son, had been sitting on the beach, weeping because of the loss of his father, when he first heard the music. He could not tell if it came from the air or the earth. Then he noticed that the sweet sound seemed to be passing by him, over the waters. It made the waves calm, and it made him feel less sad. He followed it. He wanted to find out where it came from. In this way, Ariel, who was making the music, brought Ferdinand to the door of Prospero's cave. By this time, Prospero and Miranda were there as well.

Miranda was very surprised when she saw the young Prince. She had lived for twelve years alone on the island with her father, so she had never seen anyone like Ferdinand before. She thought men always had grey hair and grey beards, like her father. Prospero asked her what she thought about Ferdinand. At first she said she did not know what he was. She thought Ferdinand was a spirit, because she did not believe a human being could be so good-looking. Then young Ferdinand saw Miranda. He was very surprised, too. At first he thought the music was being played for her, and that she must be a goddess of the island.

Miranda and Ferdinand fell in love immediately. Prospero was pleased about this, for he had planned that they should be married. However, he decided to test the strength of their love.

He spoke very roughly to Ferdinand. He picked a quarrel with him and called him a thief. He said he thought Ferdinand had come there to take the island away from him. Prospero told Miranda that she should not speak to Ferdinand, because he was someone who would steal their wonderful island from them. He also said that he was going to tie Ferdinand up by his neck and feet, give him sea water to drink, and very poor food to eat.

Miranda was very unhappy. Ferdinand was the first young man she had ever seen, and now her father was being unkind to him. She asked her father not to be so hard on him. To her, Ferdinand seemed to be a fine, brave young nobleman, who was not afraid of anything. But Prospero said that there were many young men in the world who were much better than Ferdinand. Miranda replied that she did not mind; she had no wish to see anyone nicer than him. But it was no good. Prospero refused to listen to his daughter, and he made Ferdinand his prisoner for a while.

## Murderers

The King, Antonio, Sebastian and their noblemen and servants had been wandering about hopelessly on the island, looking for food and a place to sleep. The noblemen tried to comfort the King, who thought his son had drowned. Some of them said that they thought they had seen Ferdinand swimming towards the shore. But none of them was very cheerful. Only Gonzalo had much to say. He was surprised to see how green the island was. He thought people could live there comfortably if they wanted to. They would never need to do any work, and their lives would be very easy.

At last, the King, Gonzalo and some of the others fell asleep. Getting away from the storm and wandering about the island had made them very tired. But Antonio and Sebastian, the King's brother, remained awake.

Antonio was still a very wicked man. He had not changed over the years. He said to Sebastian that as Ferdinand, the King's son, was dead, Sebastian would become the King of Naples when Alonso died. If they killed the King now, Sebastian could become King of Naples immediately. They agreed to help one another, and took out their swords. They were going to kill both Alonso and Gonzalo.

Just in time, Ariel, who was standing close by them watching what was happening, made a noise in Gonzalo's ear and woke him up. Gonzalo saw Sebastian and Antonio standing close to him and the King with swords in their hands. He asked them what they were doing, and they said they had heard a noise and thought there might be some danger. They said they were protecting the King and Gonzalo.

Prospero had commanded Ariel to look after the noblemen, but he had also told him to make them suffer for their evil deeds in Italy. When the King and his friends had woken up, Ariel tricked and puzzled and frightened them with strange sights and sounds. They began searching for food again. Just as they were losing hope, they heard the sound of peculiar music. Spirits appeared before them, in strange shapes,

carrying rich food. The spirits
invited the travellers to eat, and
then they disappeared. The
hungry men were surprised and
5  delighted, and began to eat.
Suddenly Ariel appeared, in the form of a great, ugly
bird. He clapped his wings over the table, and the
feast disappeared. Ariel himself remained before the
shocked men, and spoke to them. He called Alonso,
10  Antonio and Sebastian 'three men of sin'. He reminded
Alonso and Antonio that they had been very wicked.
He said they were hardly fit to live, for they had sent

away the good Prospero from Milan. Without any
cause, they had left him and his innocent child in a
dangerous boat. Now they themselves knew all about
the danger of storms at sea, and the sea had taken
Alonso's dear son from him. Only one thing could   5
save them from death on this island: sorrow for their
evil deeds, and a desire to live a better life in the
future.

As soon as Ariel had finished, he vanished. The
King and his friends were too surprised to speak.   10
Alonso was very shocked, for he thought he had heard
Ariel say that Ferdinand was dead. He, Antonio and
Sebastian at last realized how wicked they had been.
They felt so unhappy and ashamed that they could not
think about anything else.   15

## Three foolish people

In a different part of the island, Caliban, Prospero's
ugly, stupid servant, met two other passengers from the
ship. They were Trinculo and Stefano. Like everyone
else, they thought they were the only ones to get away   20
from the ship alive. They were surprised to meet
Caliban, because they also thought no one lived on the
island. At first they did not know if he was human or
not, he looked so strange and ugly.

Caliban was surprised to meet them, too. The only   25
people he had ever seen before were his mother, and
Prospero and Miranda. Stefano had found some wine
from the ship, and he gave some of it to Caliban to
drink. Caliban thought the wine tasted good. He also
thought Stefano was very kind to give it to him. Soon   30
Stefano, Trinculo and Caliban had drunk so much wine
that they started singing noisy songs, and behaving
very foolishly.

Caliban hated Prospero. He thought Prospero had stolen the island from him, and was very cruel to him. Caliban liked Stefano and the wine so much that he decided to serve Stefano as his lord from then on. He told Stefano and Trinculo about Prospero and Miranda, and persuaded Stefano to kill the old magician. He said Stefano would then be king of the island, and he could have Miranda as his queen. Stefano and Trinculo both thought Caliban was a strange and stupid person, but they seemed interested in his ideas. Caliban was very happy — he believed he was free of Prospero at last. He was so happy, he asked Stefano to sing a song with him.

Stefano, Trinculo and Caliban all sang together, but suddenly they stopped. They could hear someone else playing some music, but there was no one else there. The tune was a different one from the one they were singing. It seemed very strange.

Caliban told the other two not to be frightened. 'This island is full of noises, sounds and sweet music,' he said. 'It is very pleasant, and never hurts anyone.'

'This will be a fine kingdom for me, then,' said Stefano. 'I shall have music and it will cost me nothing.'

Then Trinculo noticed that the music seemed to be moving away from them, and they decided to follow it.

Of course, the music was being played by Ariel. He had heard everything they had said, and was now going to make them follow him all around the island.

## At Prospero's cave

Prospero did not keep Prince Ferdinand tied up for long, but he did give him a tiring job to do. He ordered him to fetch a lot of heavy logs and place them together close to the door of Prospero's cave. Miranda could not

understand her father's behaviour, and thought he was
being very cruel. She sat nearby while Ferdinand, who
had never had to do this sort of work before, worked
hard. Prospero pretended to go away to read, but he
watched them secretly and listened to
their conversation.

5

Soon Ferdinand was very
tired. Miranda said he should not work so hard.

'My father is in his room, and will be reading his
books for three hours more. Please rest,' she said. But
Ferdinand was afraid to disobey Prospero. He hoped
the old man would allow him to marry Miranda if he
did the work well.

10

'I dare not rest. I must finish the work for your father first,' he said.

But Miranda still wanted to help him, and she made another suggestion. 'If you will sit down, I will carry your logs for a while.'

Ferdinand would not agree to let her do such hard work while he sat and rested. He continued to carry the logs to the cave, and they talked to one another all the time.

Prospero was pleased when he heard the things that Miranda and Ferdinand were saying to one another. He was sure that they really loved each other. So the old man appeared before them, and told them that he would soon allow them to marry. He explained to Ferdinand that he had only been unkind to him to be sure that he really loved Miranda. Prospero told the Prince he could stop working.

By this time, Ariel had returned. Prospero ordered him to do something very special for the young pair. The little spirit then made the goddesses Iris and Ceres appear and later Juno, greatest of all the goddesses. These wonderful-looking people sang to Miranda and Ferdinand. Then some more spirits came and danced in front of them. The dance was very joyful until the very last moment. It ended in confusion when the spirits suddenly stopped their dance, and vanished. This was because at that moment, Prospero had heard, from Ariel, about the plot thought up by Caliban, Stefano and Trinculo. Prospero now knew that the three were coming to murder him, so he went to make some preparations.

When Caliban, Stefano and Trinculo arrived at Prospero's cave, they were all in a very bad temper. Ariel, playing his beautiful music, had led them through all the roughest parts of the island. They had fallen down into dark holes in the ground, and pools of muddy water. They were wet, dirty and tired, and they smelt very bad.

Caliban got very angry because the other two would not keep quiet. They spoke to each other very noisily. Caliban thought they would soon be discovered, and then they would not be able to murder Prospero. But Stefano and Trinculo took no notice of Caliban. They found some silver clothes hanging on a line. Prospero had left them there. When they saw them, they stopped feeling so angry. They liked these clothes very much and began putting them on, joking about it at the same time.

Suddenly they heard the noise of some hunters coming. A few seconds later, a large number of spirits rushed towards them. The spirits looked like hunters on horses, and there were many more spirits with them, looking like hunting dogs. They all chased after Caliban, Stefano and Trinculo, and bit them whenever they caught them. The three ran away in great fear, shouting and screaming as they went. That was the end of the plan to kill Prospero and make Stefano the king of the island.

## Leaving the island

Prospero, who only wanted to make his enemies sorry, now ordered Ariel to send the King and his friends to him. Ariel led them to the old man. At first, neither Antonio nor his brother, nor any of the others with them, recognized Prospero, who was dressed in his magic clothes. They had no idea that the man they saw was the old ruler of Milan. Prospero reminded them of the cruel way they had treated him and his daughter in the past. Then he took off his magic clothes,

and they saw he was
their old ruler. Alonso and
Antonio both told Prospero
that they were sorry. They promised
5  to give him back his position as ruler of Milan, and
prayed to him to forgive them. The old man did forgive
them for all their crimes and welcomed them as friends.

The old man then turned to Alonso and said,
'Because you have given me back my kingdom, I will
10  show you something that will give you as much joy.' He
stood back, and there, a little way behind him, Alonso
saw his son, sitting with Miranda. The father and son
were both delighted to see each other alive and well.
When he saw Miranda, Alonso, like Ferdinand, thought
15  she must be a goddess.

'No,' replied Ferdinand, smiling at his father. 'She is
not a goddess, but human like the rest of us. But the
gods have allowed her to be my wife. She is the
daughter of the ruler of Milan. After our marriage, he
20  will be my father also.'

Alonso replied, 'Then that marriage will make me her father, too. So I must ask my daughter to forgive me for my crime against her father.'

Prospero said they should all forget the past, and that night, he gave a feast. Caliban, his slave, served the 5 guests. Everyone was very surprised by the sight of this ugly creature.

The King and his friends wondered how they would be able to get back to Italy. Only Prospero and Miranda knew that the travellers' ship had not been destroyed, 10 and that the sailors had not been drowned. Ariel had done his work well — all the sailors were safe, and the ship was whole. As they were talking at the feast, Gonzalo saw some sailors coming towards them. The men were delighted to see that all their royal 15 passengers were alive, and Prospero's new friends were relieved to hear that the ship was still safe and strong.

'Tonight you must rest here,' said Prospero to his friends, 'and I will amuse you with the interesting story of my life after I left Italy. Tomorrow, I will show you 20 your ship, and we will set off for Naples. In Naples, Ferdinand and Miranda will be married. Afterwards, I hope to return to Milan, and to rule there till I die.'

The next day, they all left the island. Prospero said goodbye to his faithful spirits, and especially to Ariel. 25 He freed Ariel to go where he liked, but the spirit asked to be allowed to stay with the ship until it reached Naples. He wanted to make sure that they all arrived home safely.

Before he left the island, Prospero buried his magic 30 books, for he had decided never to use his magic powers again. His wishes had all come true — he was friends with his brother again, he would live and rule in Milan again and his daughter would be Queen of Naples. He did not need magic any more. 35

# 4

# Hamlet

## The unhappy Prince

When the King of Denmark died suddenly, the life of his son, the young Prince Hamlet, changed completely. Hamlet had loved his father, a kind and popular king. When he died, the Prince was terribly upset. He became even more upset when his mother, Queen Gertrude, married again, less than two months afterwards. The man she married was the old King's brother, Claudius.

Prince Hamlet was shocked and angry at this. He would never accept his uncle, Claudius, as his new father. He could not understand how his mother could love him. Claudius had no concern for the feelings of other people; he did not care at all. Compared to Hamlet's father, Claudius was a foolish, ugly man. When the Prince saw his mother and Claudius so happy together, he was very angry. It was as if her tears at the old King's death had all been lies. Hamlet could not forgive her for forgetting his father so quickly. Were all women so quick to forget the men they once loved?

Hamlet could not think of anything but his father's death and the marriage of his mother to Claudius. Nothing else seemed important. Even his dear friend, Horatio, could not make him forget it for more than a moment. Hamlet refused to stop wearing black clothes, in memory of his father's death, even after everyone else had stopped wearing them. Everyone noticed Hamlet's behaviour, and this worried Gertrude and Claudius. They hated to see Hamlet come before them, dressed from head to toe in black, and looking so unhappy. He reminded them continually of his father's death, which, for different reasons, they both wanted to forget. Because of this, the new King and his Queen asked Hamlet to come and see them at court.

'Dear son, try to forget about the past,' his mother said. 'Everyone has to die some time, you know. Don't make yourself even more unhappy.'

His uncle followed Gertrude's loving words with a long and clever speech. 'Young Hamlet,' he said, 'too much unhappiness at someone's death is foolish. Only children behave that way. Face facts — since the beginning of time, every son has lost his father. That is the way of life. And now, Hamlet, you have a new father. Believe me, I love you like my own son. In front of all these important people, I say this: you will become king after me. My boy, we are worried about you. So we do not want you to go back to university in Wittenberg, as you planned. Your mother and I would like you to be a good son to your parents, and stay here with us.'

Hamlet ignored Claudius, but told his mother he would stay if she wanted him to.

Despite the King and Queen's concern, Hamlet felt as if he were trapped. Suddenly the world was full of unpleasantness. There was nothing good left in it. It seemed to him that everyone around him was lying and cheating. He wanted to die. Why should he live? Everything seemed so hopeless. To think that his own mother could be so unfeeling. If only there was something he could do! Just as Hamlet was thinking this, his friend Horatio came to speak to him.

'My Lord, a very strange thing has happened!' he cried. 'The castle guards saw a ghost last night, and I was with them. There is no doubt about it, My Lord, it was your father!'

'My father's ghost!' Hamlet exclaimed, very excited. 'Something must be very wrong — something important. I'll speak to the ghost myself, this very evening.'

## 5 The ghost's secret

That evening, Hamlet, Horatio and one of the soldiers met at midnight to watch for the ghost. The night was dark, cold and quiet. In the distance they could hear the sound of music and laughter. The King and Queen were enjoying a feast. Suddenly, Horatio touched Hamlet on the arm.

'Look, My Lord,' he whispered, 'look, it is coming.' The ghost had appeared again.

Hamlet knew at once that it was his father's ghost. He was both frightened and curious. 'Why have you left your grave? What does this mean? What should we do? Oh, answer me!' he cried.

But the ghost did not answer. Instead, it silently signalled to Hamlet to follow it. Horatio was afraid and begged Hamlet not to go, but Hamlet fiercely pushed his friend away. Nothing would stop the Prince from following the ghost, even if it led him to hell itself. He disappeared from Horatio's sight into the black night.

When Hamlet and the ghost were alone, the ghost turned to him and spoke. What he said filled the young man with horror. He told him that he was the dead King's ghost, and that he had been cruelly murdered. 'Hamlet,' he continued, 'they said a snake bit me in the garden, but the snake that killed me now rules my kingdom.'

'My uncle?' Hamlet asked, eagerly. The look of terrible sorrow on the ghost's face told him that he had guessed correctly. 'I knew it!' the Prince exclaimed. Claudius had murdered his own brother. He had wanted both to be king, and to marry Gertrude. While the old King was sleeping in the garden one day, Claudius had crept up and poured poison in his ears. It was a horrible death.

'And now, son, your dear father is unable to get to heaven. I died before I could pray for forgiveness, and now I must burn! I command you, if you are my son, you must get revenge for this terrible murder. Help me to find peace. But,' the ghost added, 'do not harm your dear mother. You must leave her to be punished by her conscience and by Heaven.' Then the ghost vanished.

'Oh God! From this moment on, I swear I will think of nothing except the ghost's command to get revenge for this murder!' Hamlet shouted to the night sky. But as Hamlet grew angrier and angrier, he could not stop thinking of his mother. Her marriage had hurt him so much. And now he had found out that she had married his father's murderer! How could he forgive her?

When Horatio ran up to Hamlet, he found the Prince was very excited. He seemed as if he was half mad. Hamlet made his friend and the guard swear never to tell anyone what had happened that night. Then he warned Horatio that from now on, he was going to pretend to be mad, and he had a good reason for it. But Hamlet didn't tell him the ghost's terrible secret.

## Hamlet's madness

Claudius was becoming more and more worried by Hamlet's behaviour. It seemed that the young man had gone mad. Gertrude was terribly upset by this. It was spoiling their happiness together. Something else was worrying Claudius. Many things that Hamlet said seemed at first to make no sense, but if you thought carefully about his words, you would understand him. A lot of what the Prince said reminded Claudius of what he had done to the old King. 'Does he know?' Claudius wondered. 'Or is it just that I feel so guilty about what I did? I must find out.' He decided to ask one of his oldest and most trusted ministers, Polonius, to help him discover the cause of Hamlet's madness. The Queen agreed with her husband's decision.

Polonius had a beautiful daughter named Ophelia. When the King and Queen asked him about Hamlet, the minister said that before his father's death, Hamlet had told Ophelia that he loved her.

'My foolish daughter believed everything he said to her, and fell in love with him, too. I am sorry to say that she allowed Hamlet to visit her alone. When I heard about this, I put a stop to it. I told her that it wasn't right for a minister's daughter to show her love for a Prince so clearly. She should have a proper respect for the Prince's high position in the world. So I ordered her to refuse to receive Hamlet's letters, and not see him again. I believe I did the right thing. Of course, the silly girl argued and cried. She believed that Hamlet would never hurt her. But her brother, Laertes, agreed with me. He knows what young men are like! In the end, Ophelia agreed to do what I commanded. But not long after this, she had a terrible shock. She was alone in her room when Hamlet rushed in, half dressed and looking as if he had seen a ghost. She told me that he didn't say a word, but stared into her face for a long time, and then left. There is no doubt about it,' said Polonius. 'That is the cause of Hamlet's madness. The Prince is mad because of my daughter!'  20

The King wanted to believe his minister, but he decided to make certain it was true. He arranged with Polonius to set a trap for Hamlet. They sent Ophelia to meet Hamlet, while the two old men hid and watched. Certainly, Hamlet acted very strangely when he saw  25 Ophelia. But was it love? He seemed terribly angry, but not because of Ophelia alone. He was angry with the whole world. 'No one can escape,' Hamlet told her. 'Everyone is evil! That's the way life is!' He shouted out his mad words and frightened Ophelia terribly.  30

He also frightened Claudius. Claudius was now sure that Hamlet was dangerous. Even if he did not know about the murder, he suspected something. And people were starting to listen to him — the mad Prince had to be stopped.  35

# The play

Why was Hamlet pretending to be mad? Why hadn't he killed Claudius at once when he'd heard the ghost's story? One reason was that he had begun to worry about
5 the ghost. Perhaps it was not really his father at all. It could be the Devil from hell. But there was another, more serious reason for Hamlet's actions. He was a quiet, thoughtful young man. He had never been very interested in fighting — he preferred to
10 read a book. It was easy for him to think about killing someone, but not at all easy for him to do it. Still, he could not forget what his father's ghost had said to him, and he knew it was too late to stop now. Claudius was suspicious already, and Hamlet couldn't even trust
15 his best friends. His home felt like a prison. There was nothing for Hamlet to do except to finish what he had already started. But could he do it?

Hamlet heard that a group of wandering actors had come to the castle. He had seen their plays before, and
20 had an idea about how to prove that Claudius was guilty of murdering his father. Hamlet spoke to one of the actors alone, and asked him if he knew a play called 'The Murder of Gonzago'. In it, a nobleman called Gonzago is poisoned in his garden by a relative.
25 Afterwards, this relative marries the dead man's widow. The actor said he knew the play.

'Tomorrow night,' Hamlet said, 'act it in front of the King and Queen, but first I want to put in a few lines of my own.'
30 Hamlet did as much as he could to make the play seem like the real murder of his father. 'When the King and Queen watch this play,' thought Hamlet, 'I'll look at their faces very carefully. If they really are guilty of murdering my father, their faces will show it.

There can be no better proof. And when the ghost's story is proved to be true, I know I will be able to carry out my revenge.'

Hamlet invited Claudius and Gertrude to see the play, and they happily accepted. They hoped that it meant that Hamlet was at last getting better and becoming interested in things again. Hamlet told Horatio what he had arranged, and asked him to watch the King and Queen.

But as he waited for the night of the play to come, Hamlet suddenly became furious with himself.

'I am a coward! Why don't I admit it — it's not just proof that I need. The truth is, I can't do it! I can't kill my own father's murderer! How can I be such a failure and a coward? Any brave man could do it and not worry about anything at all!' he said to himself. 'Such a simple thing, and I can't do it. This is all becoming too difficult. I hate myself and I hate what I have to do. I'll kill myself! Then everything will be over, and I won't have to struggle any more. I can just sleep. But what's waiting for me after death could be even worse than this. Oh, I'm too much of a coward even to kill myself, let alone the King. There's no hope for me.' Hamlet sat with his head in his hands, waiting for the play to begin.

It was soon time for the play. Claudius and Gertrude entered, and sat down in front of the stage. Hamlet and Horatio sat at one side where they could see the King and Queen. The play started with Gonzago and his wife talking. She promised faithfully that she would never marry again if her husband died. 'Only those women who have killed the first husband marry a second,' she said. Hamlet saw his mother's face become pale.

Before the next scene, Hamlet explained to Claudius and his mother what would happen. 'You will see that

a nobleman called Lucianus poisons Gonzago in order
to get his lands for himself,' the Prince said. 'Then we
find out he loves Gonzago's wife.'

Claudius only watched a little of this scene. He
suddenly got up and rushed from the room. Hamlet had
his proof. There could be no more delay. As Hamlet
discussed what had just happened with Horatio, a
messenger told him that the Queen wished to see him
immediately.

## The death of Polonius

Gertrude had decided to speak to her son alone to try to
discover what was making him behave so strangely. But
Claudius was worried that Gertrude might discover the
truth about the murder, so he sent Polonius to find out
what the son would say to his mother. Gertrude thought
Polonius had come to help her.

Hamlet knew he had to kill his uncle. Claudius
would certainly try to get rid of anyone who knew what
he had done, even if it meant that his new son had to
die. But even when Hamlet dreamt of spilling the
King's blood, he couldn't help thinking about his
mother. He felt so angry and violent that he was afraid
he might hurt her too. He couldn't help hating her for
what she had done, but he tried to control his feelings.
'I will speak cruelly to her, but I will not use my sword,'
he said to himself.

On his way to Gertrude's room, Hamlet saw
Claudius, alone, kneeling down to pray. He could have
killed him then without difficulty. There were no guards
nearby. Claudius would not see Hamlet until it was too
late. Hamlet knew that he had to kill his uncle, and just
then, at the terrible hour of midnight, he felt he could do
it. However, he also knew that if he killed Claudius

while he was praying, that evil murderer would go straight to heaven. Hamlet's own dear father was still suffering because he had died without being able to pray for forgiveness. 'No,' decided Hamlet, 'there will be no forgiveness for my uncle. I'll kill him when he's just committed a sin. Then he'll never get to heaven.' He put away his sword and quietly left the room.

When Hamlet came to his mother's room, Gertrude told Polonius to go and hide behind a curtain. Her son's behaviour was by now so strange that she was quite afraid.

After all this excitement, Hamlet could hardly stop himself from hurting his mother when he entered her room. When he saw her, he was overcome by anger. All the terrible things that were happening now were her fault for not loving his father enough.

'So, what do you want?' he said, rudely.

'Hamlet, I'm very unhappy with your behaviour. You have shocked your father very much.'

'No, Mother dear, you have shocked my father very much,' Hamlet said angrily. How could his mother speak to him as if Claudius was his father, and her first husband had never existed?

'Come, come, you are not answering me seriously,' exclaimed Gertrude.

'Go, go — you are questioning me wickedly!' cried Hamlet.

'Why, Hamlet. Have you forgotten who I am?' Gertrude said. She was terribly shocked.

'Of course not. You are the Queen. You are your husband's brother's wife. Unfortunately, you are also my mother, although I wish you weren't.'

Gertrude had heard enough. She tried to leave the room but Hamlet stopped her. He took hold of her wrists and forced her to sit down.

'Sit down here, in front of this mirror,' he shouted. 'Look hard at yourself. I will not let you go until you see all the evil you have done.'

Gertrude was terrified. Her son was so strange and violent. 'He's going to kill me!' she screamed. 'Help! Help!' Polonius, who was still behind the curtain, heard her cries. He also began shouting for help. Hamlet rushed across the room to the curtains, realizing that someone was hiding there. He thought it was the King! 'Ah, there's a rat there!' he shouted out, and pushed his sword hard through the thick curtain and through the body of the man behind it. Polonius was killed immediately. The dead man fell from behind the curtain into the room.

'Oh, what a wicked, terrible thing you have done!' cried his mother.

'Is it as wicked and terrible a thing as killing a king and marrying his brother?' cried Hamlet.

Gertrude was horrified. What was her son saying? '"Killing a king!" What did you say?' she asked.

## The King's plan

Hamlet was shaking with anger. 'Mother, you've forgotten my father, who loved you so much. Think of my dear, gentle father and remember how good and kind he was. Look here at his picture and compare his face to that of Claudius. How can you still say you love Claudius? What is it that has made you so blind? You are too old to fall madly in love at your age, Mother.'

'Oh, be quiet, Hamlet!' cried Gertrude, putting her hands over her ears. He was making her think about things she would rather ignore. And now he was saying that Claudius, whom she loved so much, was a wicked murderer! 'Don't say any more, Hamlet — I can't bear to hear it!'

Suddenly, Hamlet stopped speaking. His father's ghost was standing in front of him. He stared at the ghost, and shouted at it, terrified. The Queen could see nothing. Now she was sure that her son was mad.

The ghost told Hamlet to leave his mother alone, as he had promised. It was angry that Hamlet had not yet killed the murderer, and urged him not to delay. Having told him this, the ghost left them alone again.

Hamlet turned to his worried mother. 'I'm only cruel to you because I want to help you. I'm really being kind,' he said.

Before he left her, he begged Gertrude not to live with Claudius as his wife any more. 'Refuse all love to the man who murdered my father and stole the kingdom. And say nothing of this to anyone.' Gertrude agreed to tell no one. But she was glad that Claudius had decided to send Hamlet abroad soon. Then, at least her son wouldn't be able to cause any more trouble. Perhaps he would even calm down and become his old self again.

Claudius had decided how he would kill Hamlet, without losing the love of his Queen and his country. He had already spoken to Hamlet and Gertrude about sending the Prince to England. Polonius's death gave him a very good excuse to do this immediately.

'Hamlet must go abroad,' he said, 'to prevent Polonius's family from taking revenge on him.'

Claudius pretended that Hamlet was being sent to England to deal with state affairs. But really the King had arranged that Hamlet would be killed as soon as he arrived in England. To make sure this happened, he gave two noblemen a letter to the King of England, asking him to kill the dangerous Prince. The two noblemen were old friends of Hamlet, so the young Prince would trust them, and be happy to travel with them.

However, Hamlet now trusted nobody, and especially not those whom Claudius had sent to travel with him. He suspected his old friends immediately. He sailed from Denmark as the King had arranged, and Claudius thought all his troubles were over, but that was far from the truth. As soon as he was alone, Hamlet searched his friends' rooms on the ship, and found the letter from Claudius. He read it with little surprise.

'So, I'm indeed surrounded by enemies,' he said to himself. 'Well, I know how to deal with my so-called friends as well as how to save myself.' Then he copied the letter, changing his own name to the names of the noblemen. As soon as they gave it to England's king, they would be killed. Hamlet was very pleased with his work. He smiled when he finished, and thought, 'I feel no sadness about the death of these men. They were quite happy to see me die. Very important things are happening now, and they were fools to get in the way.' He closed up the new letter and put it back where the old one had been.

The next day, the ship was attacked by pirates. Hamlet was the bravest fighter on the Danish ship. He jumped onto the pirates' ship and fought them alone, while his own ship escaped.

Hamlet was left with the pirates, and was sure they would kill him. But they admired his courage, and when they found out that he was a prince, they decided to take him home, hoping to be rewarded for their kindness. They sailed towards Denmark and let Hamlet land at the first port they came to.

## A new grave

As soon as he landed, Hamlet wrote a letter to his uncle, telling him that he was in Denmark again, and that they would soon meet. He did not mention that he had discovered the letter. Then he sent a letter to Horatio, telling him what had happened, and asking him to come to meet him as quickly as possible. When they met, Hamlet told Horatio about Claudius's plan to kill him.

As they were returning together to the King's palace, they saw two workmen digging a grave for a woman who had just died. Hamlet and Horatio stopped and talked to the men, who were cheerful and joking in spite of the work they were doing. As they talked together, men and women began to arrive for the funeral.

Hamlet and his friend became very curious when they saw the King and Queen among the funeral guests. There were other noblemen there too, including Laertes, Ophelia's brother. They hid themselves and watched as the priest conducted the funeral service. The priest said that he could not say all the usual prayers for the dead woman because she had probably killed herself. Laertes stepped forward.

'You devil of a priest! She was so kind and good that she will go straight to heaven!' he cried. 'Oh, my poor sister!'

When he heard this, Hamlet's face turned white.

'Is it my darling Ophelia in the cold earth?' he gasped. He felt that his heart was breaking. Silently, he watched the Queen throw flowers onto the grave. He heard her say that she had hoped Ophelia would be Hamlet's wife. He heard Laertes, full of sadness and anger, shout out — he saw him leap into the grave. And then, suddenly, Hamlet could control himself no longer. He rushed forward, and jumped into the grave beside Laertes.

'I loved Ophelia! Forty thousand brothers couldn't love her more! If you'll be buried alive with her, then so will I.'

Ophelia had heard that Hamlet had killed her father, and she had gone mad. Soon after, she was found drowned in the river. Laertes thought Hamlet was responsible for his sister's death as well as for his father's. The two men fought together in the grave and had to be forced away from each other. The funeral ended, but Laertes was determined that there would soon be another — Hamlet's.

The King realized that he could use Laertes's anger and sorrow for his own purposes. He asked Laertes to come to see him alone. Then he encouraged him to take revenge for the killing of his father. Laertes did not need much encouragement.

'I would cut Hamlet's throat in a church, if I had to!' he shouted. The King suggested an idea of his own instead.

'My plan is for you to challenge Hamlet to a friendly sword fight between yourself and him. During the fight, you will use a sword with a sharp point, not the blunt sword usually used in friendly matches.'

'A good plan indeed, My Lord! And to make quite certain that Hamlet dies when he is hit, let's put poison on my sword,' cried Laertes.

The King was pleased with this. 'We must think hard about how to carry it out. You'll have only this one chance to kill Hamlet. You should have a second plan, in case the first one fails. This shall be it — I'll have two bowls of wine near me on the table. One will contain poison. I'll wish Hamlet success in the match by drinking from one bowl, but then I'll give him the other one to drink. That way, he's sure to die, either by the poisoned sword or from the poisoned wine.'

'Polonius and Ophelia, sleep peacefully! You will have your revenge!' shouted Laertes.

'And I will be safe at last,' thought Claudius.

## The truth is known

Hamlet agreed quite happily to take part in the fighting match. He was eager to test his skill, as he had been practising. The Queen and all the noblemen gathered to
5 watch the fight. Before it began, Hamlet spoke quietly to Laertes.

'I'm so sorry for the unhappiness I've caused you,' he said. 'Believe me, I never wanted to hurt you. I love you like a brother.' Laertes looked into Hamlet's eyes,
10 and suddenly felt very sorry for what he was going to do. He thanked Hamlet for his kind words, and they shook hands. The fight began. At first Hamlet seemed to be winning. He hit Laertes with his sword, but of course Hamlet's sword was blunt, so Laertes wasn't
15 hurt. When they stopped to rest, Claudius urged Hamlet to take a drink of wine.

'Come on, dear Prince,' he said. 'I'll drink to your health. Take this bowl, and drink to mine!'

'I'll drink later, when the match is over,' replied
20 Hamlet, and put down the poisoned bowl. The fight began again. The two men fought hard. Hamlet was becoming tired. Laertes almost hit him again and again. Claudius was so excited he could hardly breathe. In a moment, it would all be over! He was watching the
25 fight so carefully that he didn't notice Gertrude get up from where she was sitting beside him. Then Laertes was hit again! The King quickly turned to Gertrude, but she was standing close to Hamlet.

'Hamlet, take my handkerchief and wipe your face. I
30 drink to your victory!' she said, and picked up the poisoned bowl.

'Gertrude — do not drink!' exclaimed Claudius, but it was too late. Claudius was horrified, but he didn't dare to say anything more. The Queen sat down again.

At that moment, Laertes cut Hamlet with his sharp sword. They struggled, and Hamlet seized Laertes's sword and cut him with it.

'Why, they are both bleeding!' exclaimed Horatio. 'Someone is cheating!'

At that moment, the Queen fell to the floor. Claudius tried to keep Hamlet away from her.

'It's the sight of blood — she has just fainted, that's all,' he said, loudly. But the Queen screamed out so that everyone could hear her: 'The drink! The drink! Oh, my dear Hamlet! The drink! The drink! I have been poisoned.' She died almost immediately.

'Someone here has done this! Lock the doors! They shall not escape,' Hamlet ordered.

'Too late! Hamlet, you're dying!' Laertes gasped, and fell to the floor. 'I'm killed by my own wickedness. My sword was poisoned, the sword you're holding now, that you hit me with. There's nothing you can do — it will take only minutes. Oh God, I'm dying! The King! The King's to blame.' Laertes lay on the ground, twisting in terrible pain.

'A poisoned sword?' Hamlet realized there wasn't a moment to lose. He rushed to Claudius and cut his arm until he bled. Then, before the guards could stop him, he seized the poisoned wine and forced it down the King's throat. 'Follow my mother!' he screamed. The King gave a horrible cry and fell to his knees. Then he fell onto the floor, face down. He was dead. Hamlet had at last taken revenge for his father's death. But he was about to die himself. Suddenly, he heard someone calling his name in a very weak voice.

'Hamlet — forgive me. I was wrong ... to blame you ... for my father ... and my dear sister, Ophelia,' whispered Laertes. Before Hamlet could answer, Laertes was dead.

By now Hamlet could hardly
breathe. His whole body was filled
with terrible, burning pain. Before his
eyes, the world was turning red and black.

5 'Horatio!' he cried, as he fell onto the ground.
Horatio rushed to his side. 'Horatio — I'm dying!
Goodbye, my poor mother! Oh Horatio, you must tell
people the truth, tell them what really happened …'

'I'll die with you, like a Roman servant when his
10 master dies. I'll drink this poisoned wine …' cried
Horatio, his tears falling onto Hamlet's face.

'No! No, Horatio, if you love me, you must suffer and
live. You must tell the world that I'm innocent. Tell
them that Claudius was a murderer!' Horatio had to
15 agree. But it was terrible for him to watch as Hamlet
twisted and screamed in pain, and finally died on the
ground before him. The young Prince of Denmark —
that good, quiet, thoughtful man — was dead.

# 5

# King Lear

## Loving daughters

Hundreds of years ago, there was a king of Britain called Lear. He ruled for many years until he was over eighty years old. Then he began to feel tired. One day, he asked all his highest ministers to come to the royal court. He also invited his three daughters: Goneril, Regan and Cordelia.

'My lords, I am tired,' he said to his ministers. 'I no longer wish to rule this country. I want to live the rest of my life peacefully and quietly, and prepare myself properly for my death.' The old man paused and looked at his daughters: Goneril, the oldest, who was married to the Duke of Albany; Regan, who was married to the Duke of Cornwall; and his youngest and favourite child, Cordelia, who was not yet married. 'Daughters,' he said, 'I am going to divide the kingdom into three parts, one for each of you to rule.' His ministers looked at each other in surprise. They were quite shocked when the King continued, 'But before I decide who gets the biggest part, I plan to find out which one of you loves me the most. Goneril, you speak first.'

Goneril was as surprised as everyone else by her father's strange request, but she just thought that he was behaving this way because he was a very old man.

'I love you more than I can say in words. I love you more than my life and more than freedom,' she said. 'I love you more than any child has ever loved her father.' The King was delighted. That was just what he wanted to hear. Pointing to a map in front of him, he drew a line round one-third of his kingdom and gave it to her.

'Now, it's Regan's turn,' the King said. Regan was determined to win as much, if not more, of the kingdom as her sister. She knew the kind of speech that would make her father happy.

'I love you quite as much as Goneril does,' she said, 'and more, for I'm only happy when I'm with you.' 'How lucky I am to have such loving children,' thought Lear, very pleased. He gave Regan one-third of his kingdom too.

'Now, little Cordelia, what have you to say to your old father?' he smiled. He wanted Cordelia to say even nicer things to him, because he loved her more than either of the others. But Cordelia knew that her sisters had lied to the old man. They had tricked their father, knowing that he was old and that his mind was no longer clear. Cordelia loved her father, but she was sure that it was wrong to use her love to win his kingdom from him. Besides, how could she explain her great love for Lear in words, without sounding as false as her sisters? She hoped her father would understand. And so, when the King asked her what she had to say, Cordelia replied, 'Nothing.'

The King was very surprised by her answer. 'She who says nothing will get nothing,' he exclaimed. How could his Cordelia say such a thing to him, and in front of all these important people? 'Have you nothing more to say, child?'

'Father, I love you as a child should love a father — no more, no less. I can't say that all my love will always be yours as my sisters have. Half my love must be for my future husband.'

Hearing this, Lear's face turned red with anger. Her cold words, compared with the sweetness of her sisters' speeches, proved only one thing to him. Cordelia did not love him. She would be punished for it.

King Lear had always had a bad temper, and it had got worse with age. 'You ungrateful girl!' he shouted, trembling with fury. 'You're no longer my daughter. I'll give you nothing — no land, no money; everything that would have been yours will be shared between my loving daughters!' He told the court his plan. The Dukes of Albany and Cornwall and their wives would rule the kingdom together. Lear would keep the title and royal position of King, and he would have one hundred noble soldiers to attend him. He would live with each of the two older daughters in turn, staying a month with Goneril and then a month with Regan.

The King's noblemen and servants did not know what to do. It was clear that the King was not behaving very wisely. In the old days, he would never have made such a poor decision. Only one man dared to risk speaking to the King in Cordelia's defence. This was the Earl of Kent, an honest nobleman. He bravely came forward, and warned Lear that he had rewarded the daughters who loved him least, and punished the one who loved him most. Lear refused to believe that he could have made such a mistake.

'How dare you question a King?' he roared. 'Get out of my sight! If you have not left this country within a week, I shall have you killed.'

Kent knew it was useless to argue. Looking at Lear, who seemed terribly unhappy despite his anger, he felt very sorry for him. He calmly accepted his punishment.

Two men, the Duke of Burgundy and the King of
5  France, had asked Lear if they could marry Cordelia. Now he had them brought before him.

'This young girl, Cordelia, is no longer my daughter, therefore I'm giving her no land and no money. Do you still want her?' he asked. Burgundy looked rather upset.
10  Without her third of the kingdom, he wasn't sure marrying Cordelia was such a good idea. However, the King of France loved Cordelia for herself. He didn't need kingdoms to persuade him to marry her. He accepted her with nothing. Cordelia loved him for it.
15  'Take her then!' shouted Lear. 'I never want to see her face again.'

Before Cordelia left for France, she spoke privately to her sisters. She begged them to take good care of their father in his old age. 'I'm sure you do not need to tell us
20  about our duty to the King,' was their proud reply. Cordelia left Britain feeling very sad. She thought she could care for her old father much better than her sisters.

## At Goneril's castle

25  Cordelia was right to be worried. It wasn't long before her sisters' true feelings began to show themselves so clearly that even the old King could see how wrong he had been. His plan had been to spend one month living with one daughter, and the next month with the other,
30  taking his hundred knights with him.

First Lear went to stay with Goneril. He soon found out how little she loved him, now that he had nothing more to give her. After a while, Goneril stopped trying to make her father feel welcome in her castle. She ordered her servants to treat him more as a poor relation than as the King. Every time she met him, she seemed to be in a bad temper.

'You complain about every little thing we do that displeases you, Father,' she said when Lear tried to speak to her. 'But you do nothing for us. Those knights of yours are always quarrelling and fighting. When I told you about this before, I thought that you would do something about it. Now I am beginning to think you enjoy seeing them behave that way. If you don't like the way things are here, then you must go to my sister, Regan.'

Soon, Lear found that his daughter had told her servants to ignore him. When he tried to give them orders, they pretended that they hadn't heard him. The King was furious. He had never been treated with such disrespect before. When he tried again to complain to his daughter, she sent him a message to say that she was ill, and refused to see him.

However, one good thing did happen during Lear's unhappy stay with Goneril. One day as he was eating dinner, a stranger came up to him and asked if he could become one of the King's servants. Lear liked the look of the man, and said he should attend him for the rest of the dinner. If at the end of the meal the stranger had proved a good servant, he could stay. He soon showed the King how useful he was. One of Goneril's servants, serving the King his dinner, was very rude to Lear. The stranger at once threw the servant out of the room. Lear was delighted. He gave the stranger some money and decided to keep him with him.

Little did the King know, this man was in fact no stranger to him. He was the Earl of Kent. Kent had been worried about what would happen to the old man now

that he had no money or power. He didn't trust Goneril
or Regan to think of their father's best interests. He had
dressed himself to look like a servant, so that he could
stay close to the King, and take care of his needs. When
5　the King asked his name, he said it was Caius.

King Lear had one other friend besides Caius: his
Fool. All kings kept fools in those days: men whose
duty was to amuse the king with jokes and songs. In
fact, the fool was allowed to speak more freely before
10　the king than almost anyone else. A clever fool could
give advice to a king, or even tell him he was wrong —
as long as he did it in a clever puzzle or a rhyme that
made the king laugh.

King Lear's Fool loved him greatly. He had tried to
15　warn Lear about Goneril and Regan, by saying that
daughters nowadays wanted obedient fathers, instead
of the other way round. He told Lear he was wrong to
give away his kingdom. Whenever Lear began to get
angry, the Fool would quickly make up a joke so that he
20　would think of something else. As many of these jokes
were about daughters who did not love their fathers,
Lear's Fool was not popular with Goneril. She could
not wait to get rid of him.

Goneril had less and less patience with her father
25　and his complaints. She began to accuse his knights of
bad behaviour again.

'Father, is there any reason for you to keep one
hundred knights and all of their servants? These men
are much too rough and unpleasant for us. Their bad
30　manners affect the whole castle. They do nothing but
eat and drink, quarrel and get drunk. They have turned
this castle into a soldier's drinking-house. Just the
shame of it should be enough to make you do
something. So please, Father, reduce the number of
35　knights a little before I do something about them

myself. And make sure that those you keep are good, quiet old men: the sort of men anyone would expect to see serving someone as old as yourself.'

Lear could not believe his ears.

'What's this? You thankless one! What lies you tell! My knights are the best in the world. They are the finest men of their kind, and they know exactly how to serve me.' Tears of anger and disappointment ran down the old man's face. He could not believe what was happening to him. He cursed Goneril as loudly as his trembling voice would let him. 'May you never have children, you unnatural creature! No, no — I hope you do have children, and that they make you as unhappy as you have made your father. I'm leaving this horrible place; I shall go and stay with Regan. Regan knows the way to treat her father the King!'

## Regan punishes Caius

Goneril's husband, the Duke of Albany, did not agree
with Goneril's behaviour, but Lear was her father and
he did not want to interfere. He came into the room as
5  the King and Goneril were quarrelling. When he heard
what had happened, he tried to calm Lear, but Lear
would not listen to him. The King called his servants,
to tell them to make preparations to leave. Then he
found out that, by Goneril's order, fifty of his one
10  hundred knights had already been sent away. Furious,
he left the Duke of Albany's castle with his servants and
the faithful Caius.

    The King decided to send Caius with a letter to tell
Regan that he was coming. But when Caius reached the
15  Duke of Cornwall's castle, he discovered that Goneril
had also written to Regan. She told her sister that she
had quarrelled with their father, and warned Regan that
their father was an impossible guest.

    After reading Goneril's letter, Regan and her
20  husband decided to go and visit the Duke of Gloucester,
rather than staying to welcome the King. Caius, still
waiting for a reply to the King's letter, followed them
there. The first person he met when he arrived at
Gloucester's castle was the servant who had been rude
25  to the King at dinner.

    Caius did not like this servant at all. He thought he
was an enemy to the King, and a coward as well. He
did everything he could to make the man fight with
him. The servant did not want to fight with the fierce
30  Caius and tried to keep away from him. But it was no
use. Soon Caius caught the servant and started beating
him.

    At that moment, Regan, Cornwall and Gloucester
arrived. 'What's this? What's going on?' the Duke of

Gloucester cried. Regan recognized Goneril's servant struggling underneath Caius.

'Punish that creature — he's beating my dear sister's servant,' she said. Some of her servants tied up Caius as a punishment. 5

'But my lady, that is the King's own messenger. The King will not like to see his own man treated in such a way,' exclaimed Gloucester, surprised.

'I'll explain everything to the King,' said Cornwall.

'My sister will like it even less, when she hears 10 that this man has beaten her messenger,' said Regan.

Her husband was not afraid of the King. He said that Caius would have to stay tied up until the middle of the following day.

**Lear meets Regan**

The first thing Lear saw when he arrived at Gloucester's 20 castle was his favourite servant, Caius, tied up. And when he entered the castle, things went from bad to worse. Furious at Caius's treatment, he angrily asked to see Regan and Cornwall. 'They are tired, after travelling all night. They cannot see you,' he was told. He made 25 such a noise after hearing this that his daughter and her husband finally appeared.

Lear immediately told Regan how badly Goneril had treated him. He had hardly finished speaking when Regan said sweetly, 'I am sure you're wrong, Father. I cannot believe that Goneril would not do her duty
5 towards you. If she complained about your knights, she must have had a good reason for it.' Seeing that Lear was about to protest, she quickly added, 'Oh, Father, you are an old man. You are in the very last years of your life. You should listen to people who understand
10 what is good for you, more than you do yourself. Please, go back to Goneril. Tell her that you know, now, that you have been unfair to her.'

'Tell her I am sorry? Is this what you think I should do?' Lear replied. And before she could stop him, Lear
15 knelt down on the floor. 'Please, dear daughter,' he said, pretending that Regan was Goneril, 'I know that I am very old. I know that I made a lot of trouble for you. On my knees I beg you to let me have some food and clothes, and somewhere to live.'

20 Regan was shocked. She asked her father to stop playing games, and to go back to Goneril.

'Never, Regan!' said Lear, standing up. 'She has taken away half my knights. She has looked at me with hateful eyes, and spoken to me with her sharp tongue.
25 I hope all of God's anger will fall on her head for being so ungrateful. I hope Heaven will strike her young bones, so that she never walks again!'

'Shame, sir, shame!' said Cornwall. He thought Lear's anger was too great.

30 'Oh, I hope Heaven's lightning will strike her wicked eyes with blinding flames. I hope the sun will burn her skin, and the air make her sick.'

Regan could not believe what she was hearing. 'Will you say the same things about me, when you are angry
35 with me?' she asked.

However, Regan had spoken so sweetly that Lear could not believe she meant to be unkind. He said he would never speak badly about her. He was just about to ask her about Caius when some visitors arrived. One of them was Goneril. Then, when Lear saw the two sisters smile at each other, he knew there was no hope for him. His daughters had become his enemies.

'Dear sister, welcome!' cried Regan. 'Now, My Lord, you can ask Goneril to forgive you, and go back to her castle until the end of the month.'

Lear refused yet again. He said he would never go to Goneril. He never wanted to see her again. He would go and stay with Regan, bringing his one hundred knights with him.

Regan began to look angry. She said that she could not allow the old King to bring more than twenty-five knights into her Castle.

'Why does he need twenty-five?' said Goneril. 'Or even ten, or five? He does not need them at all when there are twice that number of servants in the house to look after him.' Regan agreed.

'I can see that neither of you will look after me unless I come to you without my knights!' cried the unhappy King. 'How wrong I was to believe you loved me the most, and not to trust Cordelia.' Lear felt as if he would burst with anger and disappointment. He shouted and cursed and swore that he would have his revenge — but the sisters knew that he could not harm them. He was just a helpless old man.

Outside, the sky grew dark and stormy. Each crash of thunder, each flash of lightning increased Lear's anger. He felt as if the gods themselves were on his side. He could not bear to shelter in the same castle as his daughters, and be treated like a fool and a beggar. In a terrible voice, he ordered his horses.

'I would rather spend the night on the moors, even in this storm, than with such women!' he cried as he left the room. Goneril and Regan looked angrily at each other.

5 'Well, if he will not listen, he must learn from the result of his own actions,' they decided, and they ordered the castle doors to be shut. They left their father out in the storm, without any shelter and with only his Fool to look after him. Gloucester was very
10 unhappy about this treatment of the King, but he did not dare to protest.

## Out in the storm

Lear and his Fool wandered lost on the dark moors. Lear's anger was by now as wild as the storm. He cried
15 and shouted at the sky, overcome by the cruelty of his daughters. He saw that his Fool was cold and wet, and he was sorry about it, but he saw very little apart from that. He hardly knew who he was any more — he was half mad. He was found like this by
20 Caius, who had escaped from the castle. Caius took the King to an old hut nearby. The Fool went in first, but ran out again almost immediately crying,
25 'A ghost! A ghost!' Inside the hut was a madman called Poor Tom. He was very pale and dirty, with big, staring
30 eyes. He was sitting talking nonsense to himself. Lear sat down beside Poor Tom.

'I can see you have daughters, sir,' he said to Poor Tom. 'Yes, you've given them all you had, and that's why you are now so poor, and so mad. What wicked creatures they are!' Lear and the madman talked quite happily to each other. It was clear by now that Lear was as mad as Poor Tom.

Suddenly, they saw a light coming towards them. It was Gloucester, who had secretly left his castle to look for the King, and take him somewhere warm and dry. Lear made him take Poor Tom too.

Soon after he returned to his own castle, Gloucester found out that the sisters were plotting to have Lear killed. He rushed back to the King to warn him.

'Take the King to Dover,' he told Caius. 'I know a safe place there where you can stay, just across the sea from France. I will send some of my own men with you to look after the King.'

When they reached Dover, Caius, who was really the Duke of Kent, set off for France immediately, leaving the King in the safe hands of Gloucester's men. As soon as he arrived, he went to tell Cordelia, now Queen of France, what had happened. Cordelia was horrified. She persuaded her husband, the King of France, to send an army to Britain to help King Lear. She wanted to make her father King of Britain again, and punish her sisters. Cordelia herself came with her army to fight for her country.

## Lear meets Cordelia again

Old King Lear was completely mad and had no idea of the great danger he was in. He escaped from the men Gloucester sent to look after him, and wandered around the countryside, singing and dancing. He didn't care who found him. Luckily it was Cordelia's own men who discovered the mad King. Lear was quickly brought to where his youngest daughter was staying.

'My poor, dear father. If only my kisses could cure the harm my sisters have done you!' she cried when she saw him. 'I can't believe my sisters could be so cruel as to send anyone so old and weak out into a stormy night. I would not have been so unkind to my enemy's dog — even if it had bitten me, I would still have let it stay in front of my fire on a night like that.'

Lear slept for a time, and woke up much calmer than before, although still very confused. At first he didn't even recognize Cordelia.

'Where am I? Who are you, and why didn't you let me die? Life is too hard for me now. I am old and foolish. Why, I almost think you are my daughter, Cordelia.'

'Father, you are right — it is me!'

'Really? But you won't love me any more. Your sisters don't love me, although they have no reason to hate me. But you, you have a reason to hate me, Cordelia,' said Lear, sadly.

'Father, I love you as much as I ever did,' Cordelia replied softly. Lear then begged her forgiveness for not trusting her at the beginning. The father and daughter were very happy to be together again. Cordelia sent her doctor to examine Lear, and he said that, with plenty of rest, the King would become much better. It seemed that everything would be all right at last.

Cornwall and Albany had heard that the King of France was attacking Britain with his armies. They and their soldiers marched to the South to meet the French. The Frenchmen fought bravely, but the British were too strong for them. France was beaten, and Lear and Cordelia were taken prisoner by Edmond, the son of the Duke of Gloucester. Edmond was a very dangerous man. He was full of hate and anger. He wanted to be king, and so secretly arranged for Lear and Cordelia to be murdered in prison.

## Sad times

As Lear and Cordelia lay in prison, strange things began to happen in the British court. Goneril and Regan became more and more cruel. When they discovered that Gloucester had helped Lear that stormy night, they put out his eyes and left him to wander blind and helpless on the moor. Then suddenly, the two sisters began to behave as if they hated each other, and no one knew the reason why. Regan's husband, the Duke of Cornwall, died.

Then the truth was discovered. Both Goneril and Regan had been as unfaithful to their husbands as to their father. They were now both in love with the same man — the evil Edmond. He had pretended to each sister that he loved only her. The sisters needed little encouragement, and soon they were both wildly in love. But when Cornwall died, Regan told Goneril that she was going to marry Edmond. Goneril realized that he had used them both in order to get power for himself. Edmond was a liar, but she still loved him and was determined not to let her sister have him. Mad with love, Goneril killed Regan.

Albany discovered what had happened. He hated the cruel creature his wife had become. Goneril herself was so sad that she killed herself soon afterwards.

A stranger came and challenged the evil Edmond to a fight. Edmond did not know who the stranger was, but he thought that he looked like a good knight, and so the two fought. After a hard struggle, the stranger showed that he was the better fighter of the two.

Edmond was defeated. He wanted to know who the stranger was. It was his brother, Edgar. Edgar told everyone all the bad things that Edmond had done, and Edmond at last felt very sorry for his wickedness. Then
5   he suddenly remembered that he had ordered one of his soldiers to kill Cordelia and Lear.

Everyone rushed to the prison to try to stop the soldier from following Edmond's orders. But they were too late. Lear came slowly out, carrying the dead body
10  of Cordelia in his arms. She had been murdered before his own eyes. Mad with anger, the King had used all his strength to kill the soldier. Now he was trying to breathe life into the dead Cordelia. But it was no
15  use. His heart was broken. He lay down beside her and died, too.

Edgar looked sadly
20  at the body of the dead King. 'These are sad times,' he said. 'Such sadness makes us say what we feel, not what we think best. The truth is that the oldest person here has suffered the most. We who are young will never see so much, or live so long as King Lear.'

# Questions and Activities

## *1*  The Merchant of Venice

*A*  *Match the beginning of each sentence to the right ending.*

1  Mercy rewards not only the man who receives it,

2  If we do not insist that this man obeys the law now, other people

3  The words of this agreement say clearly that Shylock

4  But if he spills a single drop of blood, then all his money

5  If anyone plans to kill a citizen of Venice, half his property

a  must be given to the State.

b  may take 'a pound of flesh'.

c  may follow his bad example.

d  must be given to that citizen.

e  but also the man who gives it.

*B*  *Circle the right words to say what happened.*

Portia took the ring from her (1) **pocket/bag**, and told Antonio to give it to Bassanio. Bassanio looked at it, and was (2) **surprised/angry** to see that it was the one he had (3) **lost/given away**. Portia then showed her (4) **husband/brother** the letter from Dr Bellario, and so he (5) **remembered/discovered** that the clever

(6) **lawyer/doctor** was really his (7) **wife/sister**. He

realized that her (8) **courage/beauty** and cleverness

had saved the (9) **money/life** of his dear friend,

Antonio. He was (10) **very sad/delighted**.


## 2   Macbeth

*A   Put the letters of these words in the right order.
The first one has been done for you.*

When Lady Macbeth read her husband's letter, she

*determined*

was (1) **meetirnded** that he should rule (2) **daSclont**.

But Macbeth would have to act without (3) **cryme**

for others. He would have to make (4) **meshlif** King,

but she was (5) **darifa** that he was too kind to do it.

She (6) **zleeraid** that she would have to (7) **regu** him

to take action. She (8) **ceddied** that Duncan must

be (9) **edruderm** while he was staying at their

(10) **tacles** that night. Macbeth was so (11) **dlevo**

and (12) **dermaid** that no one would think he had

done it.

*B    Who did these things? Fill in the gaps with the
names from the box. You can use some names more
than once.*

| | | |
|---|---|---|
| Donalbain | Macbeth | Malcolm |
| Lady Macbeth | Macduff | |

**1** ................................. went straight to the King's
room and killed his two servants.

**2** ................................. and ................................. decided
to run away, one to England and one to Ireland.

**3** ................................. paid men to kill Banquo and
Fleance when they were out riding.

**4** ................................. left his home suddenly and
went to England to join Malcolm.

**5** ................................. gathered an army in England to
defeat Macbeth, so he could be King.

**6** ................................. walked about the castle in her
sleep, talking wildly about the murder.

**7** ................................. told his men to carry branches
as they marched through Birnam Wood.

**8** ................................. killed King Macbeth, cut off his
head, and presented it to Malcolm.

## *3* **The Tempest**

*A* *Put these sentences in the right order. The first one has been done for you.*

1 The servants of Antonio and Alonso seized Prospero and Miranda in Milan. ‖1‖

2 But Prospero and Miranda did not drown, and sailed for many days across the waters. ☐

3 Every day he studied his books until he became skilful in magic. ☐

4 Then they made them get into an old boat, and left them. ☐

5 Prospero found a large, dry cave on the island, and put his books in there. ☐

6 Next, the servants put them in a ship, and took them far out to sea. ☐

7 In the end, the boat brought them to a strange and mysterious island. ☐

*B* *The underlined sentences are all in the wrong paragraph. Which paragraph should they go in?*

1 Ferdinand followed the sound of sweet music to the door of Prospero's cave. <u>Miranda tried to help Ferdinand, but he would not let her.</u> Miranda and Ferdinand fell in love immediately. ☐

2 Prospero decided to test the strength of their love. <u>Miranda was very surprised because she had never seen anyone like him before.</u> Miranda was very unhappy that her father was so unkind to Ferdinand. ☐

**3** Then Prospero ordered Ferdinand to fetch a lot of heavy logs. <u>He picked a quarrel and called Ferdinand a thief.</u> When Prospero heard what they said, he was sure they really loved each other.

## **4** Hamlet

*A Who said these things? You can use some names more than once.*

| | | |
|---|---|---|
| Claudius | Horatio | Polonius |
| Gonzago's wife | the King's ghost | Queen Gertrude |
| Hamlet | Laertes | |

**1** 'Too much unhappiness at someone's death is foolish.'

**2** 'The castle guards saw a ghost last night — it was your father!'

**3** 'The snake that killed me now rules my kingdom.'

**4** 'The Prince is mad because of my daughter.'

**5** 'I'm too much of a coward to kill myself, let alone the King.'

**6** 'Only those women who have killed the first husband marry a second.'

**7** 'Don't say any more, Hamlet — I can't bear to hear it.'

**8** 'I'm only being cruel to you
  because I want to help you.'

**9** 'I loved Ophelia! Forty
  thousand brothers couldn't
  love her more!'

**10** 'I would cut Hamlet's throat
  in a church, if I had to!'

**B**   *There are ten mistakes in this description of the
fight between Hamlet and Laertes. Find and correct
them.*

The fight began. At first Hamlet seemed to be losing.

He hit Laertes with his stick, but of course it was

old, so Laertes wasn't hurt. The two men fought

hard. Hamlet was becoming excited. Claudius was so

sad he could hardly breathe. In an hour, it would all

be over! Then Laertes cut Hamlet with his blunt

sword. They struggled, and Hamlet dropped Laertes'

sword and cut him with it. Only Laertes was

bleeding. No one was cheating!

## 5 King Lear

*A    Which of these sentences are true? What is wrong with the false ones?*

|  | T | F |
|---|---|---|
| **1** King Lear ruled Britain until he was over ninety years old. | ☐ | ☐ |
| **2** Then he decided to divide up the kingdom for his three daughters to rule. | ☐ | ☐ |
| **3** But first he didn't want to find out which daughter loved him the most. | ☐ | ☐ |
| **4** Goneril and Regan both told King Lear that they did not love him. | ☐ | ☐ |
| **5** Cordelia said that she loved Lear as a child should love a father. | ☐ | ☐ |
| **6** Her warm words proved only one thing to Lear — that she loved him. | ☐ | ☐ |
| **7** He decided to share everything between Goneril and Regan. | ☐ | ☐ |
| **8** Lear would keep the title of King, and live with Cordelia and Regan. | ☐ | ☐ |

*B    Fill in the gaps with the words from the box.*

| | | | |
|---|---|---|---|
| beside | cruelty | found | nonsense |
| clear | dark | happily | wild |
| cried | escaped | madman | |

Lear and his Fool wandered lost on the

(1)        moors. Lear's anger was as

(2)        as the storm. He (3)        and

shouted at the sky, overcome by the (4) ▨▨▨
of his daughters. He hardly knew who he was any
more. He was (5) ▨▨▨ like this by Caius,
who had (6) ▨▨▨ from the castle. Caius
took the King to an old hut. Inside the hut was a
(7) ▨▨▨ called Poor Tom. He was sitting
talking (8) ▨▨▨ to himself. Lear sat down
(9) ▨▨▨ him. They talked quite
(10) ▨▨▨ to each other. It was (11) ▨▨▨
by now that Lear was as mad as Poor Tom.

## Whole book

*Match the person to the right description.*

| | | | | |
|---|---|---|---|---|
| 1 | **Nerissa** | • | • **a** | Told Macbeth that he would become king. |
| 2 | **Edmond** | • | • **b** | The ugly son of the witch, Sycorax. |
| 3 | **Ophelia** | • | • **c** | Gloucester's evil son, who wanted to be king. |
| 4 | **Caliban** | • | • **d** | The chief spirit on Prospero's island. |
| 5 | **Three witches** | • | • **e** | Portia's servant, married to Gratiano. |
| 6 | **Ariel** | • | • **f** | Went mad, and drowned in a river. |

# Book Report

*Now write a book report to display in the library or your classroom. These questions will help you.*

**Title**

**Type**  What type of story is your book?

- Adventure
- Classic
- Crime
- Detective story
- Fairy tale
- Horror and suspense
- Mystery
- Play
- Romance
- Science fiction and fantasy
- Short story
- Others

**Characters**        Who are the main characters in the book?

**Main characters**   Describe the main characters.
                      What do they look like?
                      What are they like?

**Story**             What is the story about?
                      Remember not to give the ending away!

**My comments**       What did you think of the story?
                      Did you enjoy it?
                      Would you recommend this book to your classmates?

Visit the website and download the book report template
**www.oupchina.com.hk/elt/oper**

## STARTER

**The Ant and the Grasshopper and Other Stories by Aesop**
Retold by David Foulds

**The Brave Little Tailor and Other Stories by the Brothers Grimm**
Retold by Katherine Mattock

**The Emperor's New Clothes and Other Stories by Hans Christian
  Andersen**
Retold by Janice Tibbetts

**Folk Tales from Around the World**
Retold by Rosemary Border

**Giants, Dragons and Other Magical Creatures**
Retold by Philip Popescu

**Heroes and Heroines**
Retold by Philip Popescu

**In the Land of the Gods**
Retold by Magnus Norberg

**Journey to the West**
Retold by Rosemary Border

**The Lion and the Mouse and Other Stories by Aesop**
Retold by David Foulds

**The Little Mermaid and Other Stories by Hans Christian Andersen**
Retold by Janice Tibbetts

**The Monkey King**
Retold by Rosemary Border

**Peter Pan**
Retold by Katherine Mattock